CHAMPIONS FOR CHANGE

HOW THE **MISSISSIPPI STATE BULLDOGS**
AND THEIR BOLD COACH DEFIED SEGREGATION

KYLE VEAZEY

Charleston · London

THE
History
PRESS

Published by The History Press
Charleston, SC 29403
www.historypress.net

Copyright © 2012 by Kyle Veazey
All rights reserved

Images courtesy of author unless otherwise noted.

First published 2012
Second printing 2012

Manufactured in the United States

ISBN 978.1.60949.608.1

Library of Congress CIP data applied for.

CONTENTS

ACKNOWLEDGEMENTS

In the spring of 2009, I was living in Starkville, Mississippi, covering Mississippi State University (MSU) sports for the *Clarion-Ledger* newspaper of Jackson. One spring evening, following a football practice, the documentary *Game of Change*, produced on the occasion of the forty-fifth anniversary of MSU's historic 1963 basketball team, was being shown on the video board at Scott Field. I stopped by and watched it, and upon leaving, I resolved to read the book about that team. After searching and searching, I soon learned that no such book existed. So, a year or so later, I decided to write it. I would not have finished it, though, without the help of so many.

I had been married to my wife, Courtnay, all of about five months when I decided to tackle this project, and she's been more than supportive in the two years since. Her loving encouragement has been essential, and I'll be forever grateful for it. Rick Cleveland, my friend and mentor from our days at the *Clarion-Ledger*, offered a substantial amount of counsel and never failed to check in on my progress. Just knowing that Rick felt I would be a good person to write this book was a humbling endorsement. Michael Lenehan, a far more accomplished writer than I'll ever be, provided support and encouragement while he worked on his book on the Loyola team. Mark Keenum, Sid Salter, Scott Stricklin, Gregg Ellis, Mike Nemeth and Joe Galbraith at Mississippi State were supportive and helpful. Michael Ballard, Amanda Carlock and Ryan Semmes of the MSU Mitchell Library Special Collections provided friendly encouragement. Ryan became particularly valuable as he patiently filled my requests to look through boxes of material in the university archives' substantial collection, and Amanda likewise patiently filled my requests for images. Jeff Roberson gladly volunteered a day to show me around his native Baldwyn. Scott Cacciola, Geoff Calkins, Wright Thompson, Mike Wyrick, Grant Gannon, Troy Jenkins, Clay Kesterson, Steve Ross and Steve Montgomery provided support, encouragement and advice. And a special thanks goes to J.D. Johnson, who decided that his role was simply to scold me every time he saw me about how far behind I was in the book. He didn't realize it at the time, but my desire to respond to his scoldings with a good answer prompted me to work even harder.

Rusty Hampton, Don Hudson and Ronnie Agnew were gracious in giving me their blessing to tackle such a lengthy side job while I worked at the *Clarion-Ledger*. David Williams, Louis Graham and Chris Peck were equally as receptive to my commitment when I came to work for the *Commercial Appeal*.

Travis Haney and Larry Williams were especially generous with their advice and their recommendations of The History Press. They were right. Will McKay has been a terrific commissioning editor. I also owe my wife and the aforementioned Rusty Hampton and David Williams for perusing my drafts and offering advice.

All of the former players and principal individuals I interviewed have been exceedingly helpful. Jimmy Wise provided counsel and support, not to mention some rich memories. I sought out Bailey Howell one fall day in 2010 if for no other reason than to get his blessing; his reception of the topic was fantastic. Leland Mitchell invited me into his home despite the physical limitations that have become a part of his later years. Larry Lee's collection of legal filings saved valuable time. Larry Templeton's counsel was valuable.

Relying on memories of events fifty years ago is not a perfect science, so it should come as no surprise that nailing down precise details often became an exercise in determining which account to assign the most credibility. (Aubrey Nichols said it best at the start of our interview: "The memory is dulled by the passage of time. Obviously, it's been somewhat amusing as we've read different stories through the years about the different recollections of the players, generally with the same theme.") In the vast majority of instances, primary accounts such as the newspaper stories from those days helped clear the confusion. As a newspaperman myself, I extend a special thanks to the work long ago of reporters such as Robert Fulton, Lee Baker and Carl Walters. In some instances, no such authoritative tiebreaker existed. In that case, I had to make my best judgments about which accounts were reliable. Most of the time, I decided that it wasn't worth attempting, no matter how much the evidence leaned one way or the other. As for those times that I did, I take full responsibility.

Chapter 1

A JOYOUS HOMECOMING

At the crossroads about ten miles east of Starkville, Mississippi, on the afternoon of February 24, 1959, scores of cars lay in wait for their conquering heroes. The Trailways bus, on the road for some six hours from New Orleans, was met with jubilation. It turned left toward Starkville, where a party was planned.

The bus contained Mississippi State University's most successful athletes in nearly two decades—the 1959 Southeastern Conference basketball champions, an honor clinched a night earlier in a fourteen-point win at Tulane. Never in the program's half century of existence had it won a conference title. Since Mississippi State joined the Southeastern Conference (SEC) as a charter member in 1932, the best it had managed in the league's basketball standings was fourth.

So yes, Starkville intended to celebrate. The bus soon became enveloped in a motorcade of Chevrolets, Fords, Plymouths and Buicks. On the two-lane highway from the junction—home to a rural watering hole that probably wasn't altogether unfamiliar to some of the bus's occupants—the parade plowed west toward its final destination: the heart of Mississippi State's campus. There, more supporters, mainly students, had gathered around the YMCA building. The bus arrived but idled for a few moments. Inside, the team's coach, Babe McCarthy, commanded his players not to walk off the bus. The championship match of a hearts tournament was being played, and the team was determined to see it through. Soon, though, the players walked off the bus and, in the cheering din, climbed the steps of the building to its

In this undated photo, a crowd of students and townspeople swarm around a bus returning a victorious Mississippi State basketball team. *Courtesy of University Archives, Mississippi State University Libraries.*

The YMCA building on Mississippi State's campus.

patio, which served as an impromptu stage. Jack Cristil, the team's young radio announcer with the booming gravelly voice, spoke. So did McCarthy. He was presented with the key to the city, and the crowd, which the papers estimated at about three thousand, roared its approval.

The celebration was not to commemorate the end of the season, which was hardly over. Four nights later, the Maroons would have to venture to enemy territory and climb those stairs up to hated Ole Miss's second-floor bandbox of a gymnasium. A win would mean an outright SEC title, one the Maroons wouldn't have to share with Auburn or Kentucky. But thanks to Mississippi State's 66–58 win over Kentucky on February 9, it had already clinched its berth into the twenty-three-team NCAA tournament that would start two weeks later. The Southeastern Conference's representative would start its play at the Mideast Regional in Evanston, Illinois, on the campus of Northwestern University. "We are only four games away from the national championship," said McCarthy, who in four short years had turned around an afterthought of a program into the fifth-best team in the country, according to the Associated Press. Up next, it could be presumed, was the quest for the national title in the NCAA tournament.

Chapter 2

CONSTRUCTING THE DYNASTY

Mississippi State's success story began in the northeast Mississippi village of Baldwyn, a town of a few thousand on the main highway a few miles north of Tupelo. Though divided by the line between Prentiss and Lee Counties, Baldwyn comes together through basketball, filling a gym that seats about eight hundred on Friday nights in the winter. Though some paint Mississippi as a football-first state, that's not the case in many of the small towns in the hill country north and east of Tupelo. In New Site, Wheeler, Walnut, Myrtle and a few dozen other dots on the map, basketball is king. In some places, football isn't even played. Baldwyn is particularly proud of its basketball, boasting state title teams and all-state players on signs on the northern end of its gym and displaying a wall full of trophies in the lobby on the other side of that wall.

Not unlike most other southern towns of its size, it has its common set of surnames. Historically, McCarthy is one of its most popular. In the early part of the twentieth century, one of the clan, Edward, opened a cotton gin and ice plant in Baldwyn. And on October 1, 1923, his wife, Florrie McCarthy, gave birth to a son they named James Harrison McCarthy.

But since he was the last of their four children, a nickname quickly took hold: Babe. In 1941, young Babe graduated from Baldwyn High School. Confident, cocksure and quick to speak, Babe McCarthy's personality was just as quick to form. He was always the center of attention. But when he laid eyes on Laverne Davis while home on leave from the air force in 1943, he couldn't muster the courage to ask her on a date. A friend served as intermediary, telling the sixteen-year-old Baldwyn High student that she had caught Babe's eye. Laverne, though, had her eye on a boy who lived across the street. Reluctantly, she agreed to go to a movie with Babe in Booneville. She fell in love with him that night.

But Babe McCarthy still owed quite a bit to Uncle Sam. So he went back overseas not long after that first date and pledged to write his new love. When he did, he signed his letters as "Jim" and not "Babe," in case a snooping fellow serviceman saw his signature and found easy teasing material. McCarthy stayed overseas for two more years, flying transport missions chiefly over what came to be known as the Burma Hump—a dangerous route over the Himalayan Mountains between India and China.

One night in 1945, McCarthy returned to his hometown on the Rebel, a passenger train on the Gulf, Mobile & Ohio Railroad that serviced Baldwyn. A year later, while McCarthy was still finishing his coursework at Mississippi State, he married the woman he couldn't get the nerve to ask on a date a few years earlier. But because Edward McCarthy forbade his children from getting married until they graduated college, and because Babe still had some time remaining, they had to elope to Pontotoc, a town about forty miles southwest of Baldwyn.

Later in 1946, Babe McCarthy graduated with his degree from Mississippi State College—and the secret marriage was secret no more. He quickly found work. His brother-in-law, Nelson Vandiver, had been the head coach at Baldwyn but was looking to leave. McCarthy, who had only dabbled in sports in high school and hadn't particularly excelled at any, took over as a civics teacher and as the head football, basketball (boys and girls) and baseball coach at Baldwyn High. It was an impossible job. McCarthy knew next to nothing about football and wasn't exactly the most studied Xs-and-Os man in basketball, either. And baseball? The job of coaching that team, especially in the late winter weeks in which it overlapped with basketball, often fell to some of the more responsible seniors on the team. By the summer of 1947, after just one year in the job, McCarthy successfully petitioned the school system to get him some help.

He asked Billy Roberson, a friend of his from the time McCarthy had helped Roberson and his Pontotoc High teammates in 1942, to be his assistant coach. But Roberson still needed one more semester at Ole Miss to get his degree and initially turned him down. "He finally talked me into it," Roberson recalled. "Babe could do that. That's the way he recruited. He would not let you say no." Roberson's acceptance came with a strict condition: It would be for one year and one year only. Instead, he started dating a pretty music teacher and never left Baldwyn.

Under McCarthy and Roberson, Baldwyn, a town always serious about its basketball, would get even more serious in the winter of 1948. Behind standout center Hoyt Wood, the Bearcats were one of the area's top teams. They would've been *the* top team if not for their archrival, Booneville, which had beaten them in both the Northeast Region and North Mississippi championship games. In the state championship tournament in Jackson, though, the Bearcats caught a break: Puckett beat Booneville in a semifinal game, clearing the path. The Bearcats defeated Hickory in the semifinal, setting up a state title game between Puckett and Baldwyn. Puckett led most of the way, but with McCarthy administering a running style, Baldwyn wore down its foe and tied the game at 30 late. Wood took over, and Baldwyn celebrated its first state title since 1932 with a 38–31 win. At the age of twenty-four, Babe McCarthy was a championship coach.

As a teacher, McCarthy carried over his slick-talking, sharp-dressing ways into the classroom. Often, he would start his civics classes with stories about his time as a pilot in the war. It was a rich mine for stories, but one stood out. One time, while flying a load of stubborn mules in his cargo hold, it became clear to McCarthy that there was too much weight shifting from side to side for his flight to end well. So he opened the hatch, and out dropped the mules, falling thousands of feet below to the Himalayans. "He would make the story come alive to us," recalled Bobby Nichols, who took one of his classes in the late 1940s. "And then, before we knew it, as he was telling the story, he was off in a civics class, see?"

In Baldwyn, Babe and Laverne started their family. Jim was born on New Year's Day 1949. Tim was born on November 27, 1950. Family or no, Baldwyn would not hold Babe McCarthy for long. McCarthy enlisted in the Air Force Reserves, thinking that he'd be committed to one weekend a month and not much more. About two months later, as operations in Korea escalated, McCarthy's unit got its call. So he packed up his wife and young children and moved to Memphis, where he coached the local air force base's basketball team. Success followed him there, too, as his squad won a Southeastern AAU tournament and finished among the top teams in all of the air force.

Once he was released from his commitment, the McCarthys returned home to Mississippi. He taught classes and coached the middle school team at Tupelo's Milam Junior High School, settling into a duplex there in that town not too far from where he was born. By this time, McCarthy had made his way into something else he loved: refereeing basketball games. But the low pay of a schoolteacher wasn't enough. By 1953 or 1954, acting on an arrangement from his neighbor in Tupelo, McCarthy had landed a job as a salesman for Standard Oil.

This meant a move to Clarksdale, a thriving town in the Mississippi Delta more than one hundred miles to the west. It felt like a world away from the place of McCarthy's youth. Steeped in the cotton trade in the nation's richest (and flattest) ground, Clarksdale felt like a different state than the hill country of northeast Mississippi. Still, the job provided more for his family and allowed him to continue to referee basketball games, a side job that he very much liked because it provided him a connection to the sport.

An hour down Highway 45 in Starkville, Mississippi State of the mid-1950s was an institution easily working its way into old age. On February 28, 1878, Governor John M. Stone signed a bill establishing the Agricultural and Mechanical College of the State of Mississippi. But the legislation didn't establish its location, setting off a year-long battle to determine the site. Meridian, Starkville and West Point were the contenders by the end of the year. Starkville, a burg with small growth due to not being on a major rail line, was chosen, and the construction of the first building started in the summer of 1879.[1] By the 1954–55 academic year, some 2,764 students were enrolled; 93 percent of them were from Mississippi.[2] Like the rest of the schools governed by Mississippi Institutions of Higher Learning, it was segregated (and until 1958, Mississippi State University was still Mississippi State College).

In athletics, the Maroons hadn't established any sort of foothold on the South's major powers. They made occasional marks, though. In 1941, State won the Southeastern Conference football title. A year earlier, State had perhaps an even better year, going 10-0-1, tying just Auburn, and advancing to the Orange Bowl. State kept up measured success through much of the 1940s under Allyn McKeen but bottomed out with a 0-8-1 season in 1949, its first season under Slick Morton. Murray Warmath brought respectability back to the program starting in 1952, and Darrell Royal was entering his second year as coach in the summer of 1955. The school's baseball team won SEC titles in 1948 and 1949.

Basketball, though, had been particularly devoid of success. Through the 1954–55 season, State played SEC basketball for twenty-two seasons. Just nine had produced overall winning records. Take away the lower-level schools on which the Maroons often feasted, and the results were even barer: State had just three winning seasons in conference games in that twenty-two-year span. Stanfield Hitt coached State to its highest-water mark in that span, a 14-8 overall mark and 13-7 league record in 1943–44, good for fourth place. But World War II meant a cancellation of the next season, and Hitt's teams in 1946 and 1947 combined to win just 10 games. Paul Gregory took over for Hitt before the 1947–48 season, but his results only added to the program's malaise. State won just 20 games in Gregory's first four seasons. State somehow managed to go 12-11 in 1951–52, but even that was misleading: State finished tenth in the twelve-team league with a 4-10 conference record. Gregory's teams hovered around the break-even mark in 1953 and 1954 before bottoming out in 1955. Even with sophomore Jim Ashmore, who was a second-team all-SEC player that year, the Maroons bumbled to a 2-12 record in the conference, their loss total also equaling their standing in the dozen-team league. Gregory had already checked out, though, announcing his resignation, effective the end of the season, by the middle of the year. That left C.R. "Dudy" Noble, who had coached both baseball and football at Mississippi State, looking for someone to run his basketball team.

It isn't well documented how an oil salesman from the Delta became the head basketball coach at a Southeastern Conference school, but that's exactly what happened in the winter of 1955. A friend of McCarthy's in Ackerman, an influential State alumnus, helped pave his way to an interview with Noble. McCarthy nailed it, and the school announced his addition on February 19, 1955.

McCarthy's hiring made very little in the way of a splash in the newspapers, which was indicative of the lack of clout the sport carried among readers. The *Jackson Daily News*, the afternoon daily in the state's capital that had statewide circulation and influence, ran just five paragraphs next to a longer notebook about the outdoors scene but above a story about the Pearl girls and Puckett boys winning the District 6-BB basketball tournament. The *Starkville News*, then a weekly periodical that was printed each Friday, carried news on its front page about an all-time record in a polio drive, the upcoming election of countywide offices and the Lions Club's annual minstrel show. On the sports page, the *News* included more about Paul Dietzel being named the new head football coach at Louisiana State.

Following is Mississippi State's news release, as printed in the *Daily News*:

> STATE COLLEGE, Miss., Feb. 19—Athletic Director C.R. Noble said today James H. (Babe) McCarthy will become basketball coach at Mississippi State on March 15. Noble said McCarthy, who now coaches at Baldwyn, Miss., high school, will begin spring basketball practice on April 1. McCarthy, an alumnus of Mississippi State, was appointed Thursday

C.R. "Dudy" Noble was Mississippi State's athletic director in the mid-1950s and was charged with finding a new head men's basketball coach in the winter of 1955. *Courtesy of University Archives, Mississippi State University Libraries.*

by the Board of Trustees. He has coached at Tupelo and Baldwyn and at the Memphis Air Force Base in 1951 and 1952 when recalled to military service. His team at Memphis won the Southeastern AAU title and finished fourth in the Air Force World Wide tournament. His 1948 Baldwyn team won the state prep championship. Paul Gregory, who has been temporary coach, will retain his post as professor of physical education.

State's own release carried either a mistake or a convenient omission. McCarthy had not coached at Baldwyn High School in half a decade, despite what the second sentence of the release says. Was the publicist careless in his timeline, or did he not want to claim that McCarthy had most recently been a salesman for Standard Oil before being given the keys to a Southeastern Conference basketball program?

The job ahead of McCarthy was daunting. At Mississippi State, history did not foreshadow greatness. The last time State had a winning Southeastern Conference record, Babe was courting sixteen-year-old Laverne Davis back in Baldwyn. But potential existed. In 1950, the basketball team moved out of a small gym on the south side of campus for a five-thousand-seat arena that cost $550,000. And unlike Darrell Royal, McCarthy's counterpart who coached the Maroons football team, he didn't have to deal with a burgeoning national power ninety miles up the road at archrival Ole Miss. While John Vaught was building a Rebel football team that would win six SEC titles and three national championships—and, most importantly, become the preferred destination for talented Mississippi prep football players—the Ole Miss basketball program plodded along in obscurity.

When McCarthy took over in 1955, Ole Miss had secured an SEC winning record just four times in its twenty-two years in the league. Under B.L. "Country" Graham, a native of Booneville, the Rebels were actually at a zenith of their powers, but that's a testament more to the poor past than to an outstanding present. Graham's teams posted winning SEC records in 1952 and 1960, but they were both just 8-6 marks that hardly spelled contender status in the SEC.

That title clearly belonged to Kentucky. The Wildcats had finished atop the league's standings in eight of the nine seasons preceding McCarthy's arrival. The missing season was 1952–53, when the Wildcats were enduring the death penalty from the National Collegiate Athletic Association (NCAA) for point shaving. Kentucky had won or shared a portion of the conference title in sixteen of the league's twenty-two seasons to date. In 1948, 1949 and 1951, the Wildcats won the NCAA tournament. And in 1946, Kentucky won the National Invitation Tournament. Under Adolph Rupp, Kentucky was not just the gold standard of SEC basketball; it had built itself into one of the nation's top programs, if not its preeminent one.

State's record against the Wildcats firmly illustrated the chasm that McCarthy inherited. Although it owned a win over the Wildcats in the 1925–26 Southern Intercollegiate Athletic Conference Tournament, State had never beaten the Wildcats while both teams were a member of the Southeastern Conference. Some of the results were downright embarrassing. In 1952, State lost 110–66.

Though known for its football, the conference still offered solid basketball in the mid-1950s. Under Harry Rabenhorst, Louisiana State University (LSU) went undefeated in league play in 1953 and 1954, advancing to the Final Four in 1953 and, despite losing a tiebreaker to Kentucky in 1954,

Babe McCarthy in 1959 with two of his top players, Bailey Howell (left) and Jerry Graves.
Courtesy of University Archives, Mississippi State University Libraries.

advancing to the tournament in 1954 when Rupp's Wildcats declined their invitation. Alabama finished a game behind Kentucky in the 1955 race, with Vanderbilt, Tulane, Tennessee and Georgia Tech perennial contenders. And at Auburn, Coach Joel Eaves was building a program around an innovative motion-based offense. The SEC of this era was Kentucky and a handful of pretenders, a list on which Mississippi State didn't even reside. McCarthy, though, had a plan to get there. It involved a tireless focus on recruiting, a focus that started even before he had been hired.

Kermit Davis, a country boy from Walnut, Mississippi, had started to garner some attention by the winter of 1955 for his abilities as a guard. He had essentially committed to Ole Miss and Graham but had yet to sign his scholarship agreement when Walnut arrived at Baldwyn High School one night for a tournament game. The referee that night was none other than Babe McCarthy, who, at least to anyone in his hometown who might recognize him that night, was simply the former coach who was off in the Delta selling oil. After that game, McCarthy approached Davis.

B.L. "Country" Graham, a Booneville native and the Ole Miss basketball coach. *Courtesy of Ole Miss Athletics.*

"Kermit, good ballgame," McCarthy told him.

"Thank you, Mr. McCarthy," Davis responded.

"Have you thought about where you're going to school?" McCarthy said.

"Yes sir, I have. I think I'm going to Ole Miss," Davis said.

"Well, I'll tell you something," McCarthy said. "There's a guy, they're going to have a new coach at Mississippi State, and he's a person that you know, he knows you, and I think you'd fit in well at Mississippi State." Davis received assurance that a friend of his would also receive a scholarship, and McCarthy handed him the sets of scholarship papers. The understanding was that they would be returned at the next day's game. Davis brought his back with his mother's signature, but not his own.

"Kermit, you didn't sign this scholarship," McCarthy said.

"No sir, Mr. McCarthy. I believe you, but I want to find out who the coach is," he said.

Knowing that he needed to blow his cover or risk losing his first recruit, McCarthy ushered Davis into the empty locker room at the gym. "Kermit, I'm going to be the coach," he told him. "Now, you can't tell anybody." On the bench in the locker room at Baldwyn High School, the same room out of which McCarthy crafted his 1948 prep state champions, he signed his first recruit. But it may have been the next bit of reconnaissance that meant more to McCarthy's ascent than anything else.

"Kermit, do you know any good players?" McCarthy said, after Davis had relieved the pressure and signed the paperwork.

"Yeah, I do, I know one—Bailey Howell at Middleton," Davis said.

"Bailey Howell at Middleton?" McCarthy said, indicating he had never heard of him.

"Yeah," Davis said.

"Well, why don't you get him to come with you?" McCarthy said.

"Well, I'll be happy to go see him," Davis said.

Kermit Davis was no stranger to the hamlet of Middleton, Tennessee, a speck on the map where a railroad intersected a state highway about five miles north of the state line. It was just eight miles north of Walnut, and the two teams carried a deep, passionate rivalry. Or at least they *did*. At one point, the rivalry grew so fierce, with fights between spectators, that the two schools simply agreed to disagree and not play each other in sports anymore.

But it went deeper than that. Davis had been born in Middleton, and he and Howell had started first grade together. Davis lived out in the country; Howell lived near the edge of town. Their families both worshipped at the local Church of Christ. They played quite a bit of basketball together, too, honing skills that would pay off in a big way the rest of their lives. Davis moved away to Memphis after the seventh grade, but his family returned to the area one year later and settled in Walnut. So it wasn't much for Davis to head up to Middleton one Sunday afternoon to see where Howell stood in his recruitment.

Howell, the lanky forward, had no shortage of offers. A Tennessee alum in the area was pushing hard for Howell to go to his alma mater. Memphis State College, a convenient hour due west of Middleton, was a rising program. Vanderbilt, with its sterling academic reputation, had offered a scholarship. But the big boy in the South's basketball scene, Kentucky, was also involved. Harry Lancaster, a Wildcats assistant coach, came to Middleton to watch Howell

play. Afterward, he met Howell and his parents and told him that UK would offer him a scholarship. Sure enough, the letter came in the mail soon after.

Howell was one of three siblings, the son of a rural mail carrier and a teacher. Middleton was as small town as it got. Howell was one of just thirty-four in his graduating class. One spring, the school tried to organize a baseball team, but it folded midway through the season because it couldn't sustain a large enough roster. (Howell played.) So, when his old friend Kermit Davis motored up Highway 15 that Sunday afternoon, the appeal of a small town and a familiar face couldn't hurt.

Bailey Howell, after arriving at Mississippi State. *Courtesy of University Archives, Mississippi State University Libraries.*

McCarthy soon put on the full-court press, making the 280-mile round trip from Starkville to Middleton with regularity. One time, presumably in an effort to show off his family man status to the humble Howells, he brought his entire family. He sent Don Blasingame, the Corinth native who would soon be the St. Louis Cardinals' starting second baseman, to impress him. He entertained Howell at the public swimming pool in Corinth.

It worked. Howell never got on the Southern Railway train to visit Knoxville, a town six hours and a time zone away. And Kentucky? Try as Lancaster might, the Wildcats' bid for Howell was crippled by the absence of Rupp, who never came to see Howell play. Howell signed with Mississippi State and Babe McCarthy, starting a relationship that would transform the lives of both men and the school for which Howell played.

The Babe McCarthy era, if anyone thought of it that way, got off to a nice start. Howard College came to Starkville on December 2, 1955, and McCarthy's team dispatched it back to Birmingham by a score of 108–65. The Maroons entered Southeastern Conference play with a 4-2 record, but McCarthy's first greeting to the league was harsh. State suffered double-digit losses to Auburn, Alabama, Georgia Tech and Vanderbilt to start SEC play, and to add insult to injury, it lost by 4 at tiny Sewanee. But McCarthy engineered a second-half turnaround, winning his first SEC game by 21 at Ole Miss on January 30, 1956. That was the first of 6 wins by the Maroons over their final ten SEC games, a span that would create some momentum of sorts heading into the next season. And while State's 12-12 overall record and 6-8 Southeastern Conference mark was hardly noteworthy, it was a considerable upgrade over a year prior, when the Maroons went 6-17 overall and 2-12 in conference games.

Howell, Davis and the other members of McCarthy's first signing class were nonfactors; NCAA rules then prevented freshmen from playing with the varsity team. But McCarthy did inherit a prime piece of the puzzle: guard Jim Ashmore. In 1955–56, after averaging 22.3 points per game, Ashmore was named a first-team all-Southeastern Conference player by the Associated Press.

In Ashmore's senior year, the Maroons started to make their move. But it wasn't all due to Ashmore. Howell, now a sophomore and eligible to play, had almost no learning curve to the rigors of varsity basketball in the SEC. McCarthy's second Mississippi State team started 7-2, with just losses on the road at Memphis State and Murray State, before entering league play. Again, the Maroons started slowly, losing by 20 at Auburn in the league opener and falling by 5 at Alabama and by 3 at home against Georgia Tech. Two nights later, a 1-point win over Vanderbilt provided the team a spark of sorts in

Jim Ashmore (right) and Bailey Howell are Mississippi State's first two basketball all-Americans. *Courtesy of University Archives, Mississippi State University Libraries.*

conference play. The Maroons followed their win over the Commodores with wins over Ole Miss, LSU and Tulane to set up a critical weekend of home games against Tennessee and Kentucky. In a two-overtime thriller, State sent the Volunteers limping away, 97–90. But the win of larger significance came two nights later when Rupp and Kentucky came to Starkville and lost, 89–81. It was Mississippi State's first win over the Wildcats in thirty-one years and improved the Maroons to 6-3 in the Southeastern Conference.

Yet McCarthy's team couldn't preserve the momentum through the grueling stretch of five road games to end the season that the SEC's seemingly devilish schedulers annually provided. Though State beat Georgia, LSU and Ole Miss, it lost at Florida and Tulane. That gave the Maroons a 9-5 record and a fourth-place finish in the conference.

But State's national stature climbed a bit, at least as much as it can after a 17-8 overall record. Ashmore became Mississippi State's first all-American, earning third-team honors from the Associated Press and the United Press International (UPI), second-team honors from Converse and first-team honors from the Helms Foundation. Likely realizing the capital that a win over Kentucky provided, State finished with a no. 15 national ranking in the Associated Press poll, marking the first time the Maroons had finished a season ranked among the nation's elite.

McCarthy's third season at Mississippi State would prove to be foundational. Now without the all-American Ashmore, McCarthy needed to prove that his own team was capable of maintaining the positive momentum that the 1956–57 season had built. Howell was a large part of that, but the supporting cast that McCarthy assembled enabled the success that was to come.

Jerry Keeton, a forward, was a central key to the puzzle. He grew up in Wheeler, just a few miles down the road from McCarthy's native Baldwyn in basketball-mad northeast Mississippi. The Wheeler teams on which he played went 57-2. In 1955, Wheeler won the state title. Like Davis, Keeton was familiar with McCarthy in large part because of the games he officiated. Keeton started to hear rumors that McCarthy was going to be the next Mississippi State coach, and Graham kept applying pressure for him to attend Ole Miss. Keeton, the son of a farmer and housewife in rural Prentiss County, chose Mississippi State chiefly because he wanted to earn a degree in civil engineering.

One particular freshman game gave McCarthy his starting point guard. Ted Usher came with his teammates from Sunflower Junior College for a game, and McCarthy was impressed. He contacted him soon after, and Usher arrived. That Ted Usher was even south of the Mason-Dixon line, much less playing in out-of-the-way Sunflower in the heart of the Mississippi Delta, was an accomplishment in itself.

Usher grew up a thousand miles away in Rochester, New York. His father left home when he was young. His mother worked at a Bausch & Lomb factory. Young Ted could play basketball and had a scholarship offer to Niagra out of Madison High, but he failed the English portion of the entrance exam and couldn't attend. His high school coach arranged a soft landing spot at Eastman Kodak, drawing a healthy paycheck and playing for the company's basketball team. But the desire to play college basketball kept at Usher. One of his teammates on the Eastman Kodak team told him that he knew the coach at Mississippi Southern, Charlie Finley, and could arrange for him to play there. Usher bit, but just before he was to leave, Finley called back to say that he didn't have room for him. Instead, he would arrange for Usher to make the team at Sunflower, a two-year school in Moorhead nearly 200 miles away from Mississippi Southern's campus in Hattiesburg but just 120 or so miles due west of Starkville.

The Maroons stoked fans' fire as never before with their sterling start to the 1957–58 season. State raced out of the gate to win its first 11 games.

Though the annual patsies like Southwestern and Howard were included in that number, it wasn't a cakewalk. State defeated Memphis State, which a year earlier had played in the NIT championship game. On December 13–14, the Maroons won a two-day tournament played in Birmingham by beating Auburn and Miami. On December 19, they beat Murray State, a team that had beaten the Maroons a year earlier. Ole Miss and Morehead State succumbed in a Christmas tournament hosted by State, and the Maroons opened league play with home wins over Auburn and Alabama to improve to 11-0.

It would not last. A seventeen-point loss at Georgia Tech in the next game tossed the cold water on the Maroons' fire and was the first of three straight losses, all on the road. At 2-3 in conference play and with only one team each season earning the league's berth, by mid-January State had already squandered a hot start into a year with almost no chance of making the program's first NCAA tournament. State rebounded with two nonconference wins and a flawless trip on the two-leg Louisiana weekend of the SEC schedule but was whipped by twenty-one and ten, respectively, on the February 8–10 jaunt to Tennessee and Kentucky. The Maroons won their last five games to put a polish on a 20-5 season, their first 20-win season in program history, and another no. 15 final national ranking.

The Maroons primed their fans for the year that was to come—and for good reason, too. It was do or die for Howell, the player who had quickly emerged as the best in the history of the program. (Before the season started, Howell was named to *Sport* magazine's all-America team.) And it was the final run for players like Keeton, Usher and Davis, whose careers to that point had already provided State supporters and students with the most exciting era of basketball in the school. McCarthy had now assembled a balanced team: Howell was the star, but Dale Fisher, Charlie Hull and Jerry Graves were fine complements in the paint. He had his point guard, Usher, and his trusted reserve, Davis.

The bigger picture presented itself well, too. Rupp's mighty Kentucky had lost four starters off last year's team, which won the national championship. Would Mississippi State be next? To have that opportunity, the Maroons would need to solve questions much more complicated than Auburn's shuffle or Ole Miss's rickety gym. State would have to navigate a complex web of the past, of political issues hard to understand and of a state embroiled in the first throes of a revolution that would change its very composition. The easiest part of earning an NCAA tournament invitation, it turned out, would be the forty minutes spent on the basketball floor.

Chapter 3

THE BREAKTHROUGH SEASON

Their team's football season once again completed without any semblance of success, Maroon fans toward the end of 1958 turned their hopes to Babe McCarthy's emerging basketball program. Lee Baker, the sports editor of the *Jackson Daily News*, wrote on the day of the season opener that Mississippi State fans were looking forward to 1958–59 "with unconcealed delight." Their early season results would do nothing to discourage.

State made easy work of its usual ho-hum nonconference opposition. Some 3,800 turned out on December 1 to watch the Maroons whip Southeastern Louisiana, 94–72. Wins over Union (by 43 points), Southwestern, Arkansas State (twice), Murray State and Morehead State by mid-December provided Mississippi State with its highest ranking yet: no. 8 in the Associated Press poll. (In that 121–78 win over Union, Bailey Howell scored 47 to break the school record of points scored in a game—a mark he previously owned with 45.)

After seven games of playing mostly teachers' colleges, the Maroons would get their shot to play on a competitive—and attentive—stage in New Orleans in the Sugar Bowl tournament. In the opener, McCarthy's team had little problem with Maryland, winning 56–45. That set up a game against a regional rival with whom Mississippi State was well familiar: Memphis State. The Tigers entered the game 7-0, and Loyola Fieldhouse would be the scene to an early-season duel not just for Mid-South supremacy but for a leg up on the national scene, too. The *Daily News* offered a succinct portrayal of Mississippi State's 73–55 win when it noted that the Maroons won with "the combination of an impenetrable zone defense and a carefully worked offense that set up good shots to produce a high degree of accuracy." The win did more than just dispatch Memphis State, and it meant more than the engraved fountain pen set presented to the winner. With the nonconference portion of the schedule completed, Mississippi State stood at 9-0. In the awards ceremony that followed the win, McCarthy explained his success by pointing at his team and saying three words: "There they are."

The undefeated, top-ten Maroons celebrated their Sugar Bowl win with a grueling road trip. On New Year's Eve, the squad loaded into cars and drove to Petal, Mississippi, a little more than one hundred miles northeast of New Orleans on U.S. Highway 11, where they practiced. On New Year's Day, as LSU wrangled a 7–0 win over Clemson in the Sugar Bowl football game at Tulane Stadium, the Maroons were in Montgomery, Alabama, for a practice at Robert E. Lee High School. By Friday, January 2, the squad had reached its destination: Auburn, Alabama, where on the next night, Mississippi State would open Southeastern Conference play against the Auburn Tigers, winners of eighteen consecutive games.

Joel Eaves, the Tigers' coach since 1949, had built a system on the Plains based around an offense called the "shuffle." Eaves developed this offensive approach based off the ideas of former Oklahoma coach Bruce Drake. His approach was so novel—and so successful—that in 1961, reporter Arlie W. Schardt of *Sports Illustrated* explained its concepts at length. In sum, *SI* noted that the Auburn Shuffle, as it would come to be known, "consists of a series of patterns that can be run continuously from either side of the court; if one play is stopped, players are already in position to begin another one without going all the way back to their original spots." The shuffle's ability to create layups—some ten to fifteen per game—proved ideal for teams that lacked top-flight height, which was an even more prized commodity in this age almost three decades before the three-point line placed greater value on sharpshooters.

"A trademark of the shuffle is the quick, direct pass that insures ball control and forces the defense to cover a wider area, thus increasing the chance of freeing someone for an easy shot," *SI* continued. "At its best, as shown on these pages, the shuffle increases the possibility of surprise by requiring almost no dribbling."[3] To defend it properly, players had to navigate a mind-boggling series of passes that brought them out of their traditional positions, created mismatches and changed seemingly every second. "Everybody, I don't care if you're 5 or 4 or 1 or 2 or 3, everybody changes position every time the ball is passed," Kermit Davis said years later. "And I don't care if you're a big man, you've got to come outside and guard a guy that's a center playing

Auburn coach Joel Eaves is taken off the floor by some of his players in this undated photo. Eaves perfected an offense called the shuffle that initially gave Mississippi State fits. *Courtesy of Auburn University Athletics.*

the two spot, breaking off." It was unorthodox for the times, so much so that Eaves would write a book on its intricacies—a book Hull later bought just because it intrigued him so much. "They ran that to perfection," Hull said later, "and we hadn't practiced against it."

But the shuffle wasn't the only difficulty McCarthy's team encountered that night in Auburn. Mississippi State's own uniforms would prove a daunting hurdle all their own. For road games that season, the Maroons had chosen to wear a gray uniform with maroon numbers and white trim. But when State arrived at the Auburn Sports Arena that night, they learned something they should've known months earlier: tri-color jerseys weren't allowed. Auburn pointed this out to the official, and State was assessed a technical foul even before the game started. The Tigers made both of their free throws and started the game up 2–0, which was no small advantage to a Mississippi State team that thrived on taking early leads and going into a stall. The game snowballed from there. Auburn made twenty-nine of its fifty-four shots—a sizzling 54 percent. State made nineteen of its seventy-one attempts—a 27 percent clip as frigid as the air outside. Even Bailey Howell, the all-American, struggled like he hadn't at any other point in his career. He scored 19 but made just seven of his twenty-seven field goal attempts. By night's end, an exasperated State looked up at a 97–66 loss to the Tigers—a whipping, really—and tried to find ways to explain what happened. The long holiday-week road trip to New Orleans, the hotels, the foreign gyms and the roadside diner food all garnered plenty of the blame. "We were just on the road, you know," Howell recalled. "Basically, we weren't ready for that game."

Said Hull, "We were really kind of worn out."

Said Jack Cristil, the radio broadcaster, "They kicked our ass all over the place. Babe said they'd never beat him again with [the shuffle]."

Regardless of the target of blame, McCarthy was presented with a team that had been humbled. No longer was Mississippi State the undefeated Sugar Bowl champions. Now it was 0-1 in the SEC, smarting from a whopping thirty-one-point loss and had Jerry Keeton hobbling from a sprained ankle. McCarthy's team hadn't been beaten that badly since a thirty-eight-point loss to Tulane in his first year as head coach, way back in 1956. To make matters worse, the Maroons couldn't head back to the familiar environs of Starkville just yet. Alabama awaited State two days later at Foster Auditorium in Tuscaloosa.

Hull knew that the team needed a pick-up. So, in a Sunday afternoon practice in Tuscaloosa, he decided that instead of laying up every close-range shot he had, he would dunk them. He was trying to send a jarring message that would wake his teammates up and get them out of their shuffle-invoked doldrums. And even though Alabama was close for a while, the Maroons eventually left with an 81–64 win. McCarthy's wise motivational tactics, aided by Hull's message, may well have saved the season. "I think Coach McCarthy had a way about him in handling everything," Davis said. "We put that loss behind us."

"That game was special," Hull said. "We easily could have folded and just gotten the heck beaten out of us. And Alabama had a heck of a ball club."

On Saturday, January 10, the Maroons accomplished a first for McCarthy: they beat Georgia Tech. The 75–67 win was State's twenty-fourth straight at home.

In Jackson that day, Ross Barnett, a sixty-year-old Jackson attorney, businessman and native of Leake County, announced his intention to run for governor in that fall's election. In a story in the *Daily News*, Barnett said that his governorship would "restore unity and harmony" in the state. He also claimed to be a "vigorous segregationist."

The win over Alabama would prove to be a momentum-builder for the Maroons. After the Georgia Tech win, State blew past Vanderbilt, 83–65, on Howell's 26, Keeton's 20 and Hull's and Graves's 17 each. When Country Graham and Ole Miss rolled into town on January 17, McCarthy offered no quarter for his northeast Mississippi friend. State demolished its archrival, 87–58.

Stepping out of conference, State had no problem with Murray State on January 24, winning 63–48. A little over a month earlier, in Murray, the Maroons had escaped with just a 1-point win. (One day earlier, the

Old Main dormitory, long a symbol of campus and at one time supposedly the largest dormitory in the world, was claimed by a massive fire.) At Ellis Auditorium in Memphis on January 29, State claimed its second win over Memphis State in the season, winning 53–52. Back in conference play, State ran its record to 6-1 with a 78–71 win over LSU on January 31 and a 55–46 victory over Tulane on February 2.

The winning streak set up a weekend of reckoning for State. It had been close before; McCarthy's early years hadn't exactly produced noncontending teams, but in order for Howell and the Bulldogs to prove that they were among the nation's elite, they would need to slay the nation's elite. Tennessee, which at 5-2 stood fourth in the league, would serve as a tough undercard when it visited on Saturday night, February 7. The Vols had whipped the Maroons 104–83 a year earlier at Alumni Gym in Knoxville. But doubtless the big attraction was heading to town two nights later: Adolph Rupp and Kentucky, the defending national champion and the nation's top-ranked team. In addition to the usual contingent of local newsmen, reporters from *Sports Illustrated*, the *Atlanta Constitution*, the *Birmingham News* and Memphis's *Commercial Appeal* planned to attend.

In Starkville, the anticipation reached a fever pitch. "It's a pity the gym couldn't accommodate twice its capacity," noted the *Starkville News*. "We're certain it would be filled for these two tremendous games. Starkville is sure getting lots of national publicity for the two upcoming games. Both will receive reams of publicity in papers throughout the nation. And for the next 72 hours, at least, we wouldn't be wrong in calling Starkville the Basketball Capital."

The Basketball Capital, as it were, lacked an ornate capitol. Mississippi State played its games at what was uncreatively dubbed the "New Gym," named that way because in 1950 it replaced a Quonset hut of a structure just down the hill. Red brick graced the entryway that faced north, allowing a vantage, for those who stepped outside for a smoke, of the Drill Field on the right and Scott Field on the left. A metal roof arched from north to south, with windows at the top. Inside, the basketball floor was laid out north–south as well. Permanent bleachers occupied the top two-thirds of the building on the east and west sides, all the way up to the skylights. Temporary bleachers stretched from where the concrete stopped almost all the way to the white sidelines. There was no proper seating in the end zones, one of which had a staircase that led in two directions from a set of double doors that led to the teams' locker rooms. It was not Madison Square Garden, Boston Garden, Chicago Stadium or any of the other famed arenas of the day. It was hardly

The front of the 1950 gym at Mississippi State, which is now named after Babe McCarthy.

even Kentucky's palatial Memorial Coliseum, which seated twelve thousand. But on winter nights in the McCarthy era, there may not have been a better home court advantage in the nation.

For the most anticipated contests, the pregame show featured a visit by McCarthy himself—and not for entertainment, either. With a largely student audience still filing in, McCarthy would take the microphone and urge the fans to squeeze in to allow more to enter. They all did what McCarthy said. "The students loved him," said Doug Hutton, who played on the early 1960s teams. "When they'd introduce the starting lineup and then introduce 'Head Coach Babe McCarthy,' he always got the biggest cheer."

"It was packed," recalled Jack Berkshire, a guard on the 1960, 1961 and 1962 teams. "They were standing up on the steps at the end, all the way up and down the other side. They were on the rafters, where the lights were. They were everywhere." Cowbells were the norm, at least in the early years. The players were sky high by the time of the opening tip, often hearing the cowbells ringing inside as they were walking over from their dorm. After McCarthy's pregame pearls, the team would bound out of the locker room, through the double doors, down the stairs and into the clanging fury of sound. "They talk about chills on your spine; it literally does that," said Jackie Wofford, a Starkville native who played on State's early 1960s teams. "It just gives you a sense of pride."

Beating Tennessee wasn't easy, but it happened. Howell scored 22 to lead the Maroons past the Vols, 52–45. At the City Auditorium in Jackson that night, Kentucky crushed Ole Miss, 97–72. Afterward, Rupp displayed a bit of arrogance, saying, "I figured our boys were looking ahead to Monday night and Mississippi State too much," after winning by 25. "But this was one of the good Mississippi teams we have played here tonight."

In Starkville, McCarthy, who didn't mind being boastful himself, crowed about how his team wasn't getting the respect it deserved. "I just don't think State is being given credit for being as good a team as it is," McCarthy said. "If we beat Kentucky, maybe it will change things, but I'll bet it won't make us no. 1 in the nation." In a poll that was released before the Tennessee game, the Associated Press had State ranked no. 11 in the country. United Press International voters had State at no. 17.

The team ranked no. 1 in the country, the Wildcats, quite literally found its entrance into Starkville to be less than hospitable. A Sunday thunderstorm forced the Wildcats' plane to circle the airport in nearby Columbus, thus delaying their arrival to State's alumni house until it was too late for the team to engage in a meaningful practice. The turbulence even made some of the Wildcats ill.

Yet the game's significance would not be marred by a queasy flight. The two teams, both 18-1 overall and 8-1 in conference play, were playing for "an almost certain berth in the NCAA tournament in March," wrote the UPI. This was nothing new to Kentucky. It had already been to the tournament nine times and had won the previous year's crown. For Mississippi State, a win over the Wildcats would pave the way to a first-ever SEC crown. The game didn't lack for star power, either. In addition to Howell, the league's leading scorer at the time with 27.9 points per game, Kentucky featured guard Johnny Cox, who was third in the league with 18.0 points per game. McCarthy gave that defensive assignment to Hull. "I don't care if he gets 35 points," McCarthy told him, "if you get 36."

Keeton's parents had a bit of a tradition for their trips to Starkville to watch their son play. They would have dinner at the campus cafeteria two or three hours before tipoff, and their son would come by with their tickets and for a brief visit. As Keeton walked to the cafeteria at the appointed time that night, he detected a low, rumbling noise. At first, he thought it was the approach of an off-schedule train pulling into the campus depot. But he soon realized that it was coming from somewhere else. "It was those rednecks over at the gym," Keeton said. "They were ready at least two hours before the game."

One fan among the 5,400 excited spectators brought an honest-to-goodness plow point and commenced to beating it with a hammer the entire

Kentucky coach Adolph Rupp (left) during an unspecified game of the era. Rupp led the Wildcats to the 1958 national championship. *Courtesy of Special Collections, University of Kentucky libraries.*

game. "It was the loudest noise that I think I have ever heard," Berkshire said. "I haven't heard anything like it since." Said Keeton, "I told somebody [to] go take that dang hammer away from that guy. *Ping! Ping!* He was hitting that metal all night long. Of course, that drove Rupp batty, because it drove me batty." In the *Daily News*, Lee Baker wrote that "the resulting 'bong' rolled out across the floor like the toll of a ship's bell."

Assisting in the fans' fury was Mississippi State doing what it failed to do at Auburn a month earlier: jump out to an early lead. The Maroons held on to a respectable 25–16 advantage at halftime. But by the time Howell fouled out with 4:24 to play, having scored 27 points, the Maroons were up a whopping 56–38. State held on to win, 66–58. The final fifteen seconds of the game were punctuated by State students chanting, "We're number one!" Without question, it was the most significant victory in Mississippi State's basketball history.

The *Daily News* breathlessly heralded the win. Sports editor Lee Baker's column came with an exaggerated dateline: "Stark-Raving-Mad-Ville, Miss." But below the fold, on the second page of sports, was a United Press International wire story with a Starkville dateline. Its headline summed up how many State fans must have felt when they walked out of the gym that night: "WILL THEY GO."

It seems strange, in this era of March Madness, billion-dollar television contracts, "One Shining Moment" video montages and such, for a program to wonder if it would accept a NCAA tournament bid. But this was Mississippi, and this was 1959. And not unlike essentially every other aspect of life in the state in this era, race was a factor.

In 1955, Jones County Junior College's football team earned an invitation to play in the Junior Rose Bowl. Its opponent? Compton College, of California, which had eight black players on its roster. The governor and governor-elect huddled but passed the buck to Jones's board of trustees. The trustees sent the team to California, where it lost, 22–13. In what the UPI would later term a "closed-door meeting" a short while later, the presidents of the state's junior colleges pledged not to send any more teams to play integrated squads. Sure enough, the next year, Pearl River Junior College received an invitation to the same game. It declined.

The "unwritten law"—that state-sponsored Mississippi schools couldn't play teams that had black players—had been around longer than that. In scouting a football game against Nevada in 1946, State coaches discovered that the team was playing black players. State athletic director Dudy Noble telegrammed Nevada's athletic director to inform him of what he termed as "the custom in the South" against playing integrated teams. Nevada's athletic board, upon hearing from Noble, voted to cancel the game. But the 1955 issue hardened the rule at a time when integration seemed on the horizon. *Brown v. Board of Education*, the landmark Supreme Court decision that proved to be the catalyst for school desegregation in the South over the next two decades, was still just about eighteen months old.

Both Ole Miss and Mississippi State soon encountered situations to test the "unwritten law." Both times, the schools succumbed to it. State's acquiescence came in a most unlikely place: Evansville, Indiana. In McCarthy's second season at State, the 1956–57 campaign, the Maroons entered a holiday tournament at the University of Evansville. On December 28, State faced a Denver team that provided a stiff contest. The Maroons won, 69–65. The next night, State was to face the host Aces for the tournament championship. As he was finishing his pregame meal, Kermit Davis got a tap on the shoulder from team manager Paul Duncan. "Come with me," he said. Davis protested, as he had not finished his steak. But by the look on Duncan's face, he could tell that something was amiss.

32

Davis went with him to the gym, where they gathered the team's uniforms and headed back to the team bus at the hotel. Word had spread back to Mississippi that Denver, the previous night's opponent, had a black player. The team was summoned home. "I guess if Babe would have said, 'Screw you,' you know, 'we're playing,' that he would have gotten fired, probably," Howell said years later. "And the president, Ben Hilbun, he didn't stand up to them, either, you know. He could have said 'Go ahead and play,' you know. And they would have probably fired him, I guess."

Hilbun had no desire to buck the status quo. Though his roots were in Jones County, in south Mississippi, essentially his entire life had been dedicated to Mississippi State. His previous roles had been as director of public relations, registrar and administrative assistant to President Fred Tom Mitchell. In 1954, Hilbun was inaugurated as Mitchell's successor, according to Michael Ballard's *Maroon and White*. When the miniature controversy that was Evansville landed on his lap, Hilbun didn't take a stand of change. A Natchez resident wrote to him a few days after the event, supporting his "stand on principle." Two days later, Hilbun responded with a self-congratulatory tone that he would adopt in most of his responses to those who wrote: "I am glad to have approval

Ben Hilbun sits next to Dudy Noble as he speaks at a 1954 football banquet. Hilbun, a Mississippi native, had given his professional life to Mississippi State. *Courtesy of University Archives, Mississippi State University Libraries.*

of my action, which makes me know that my decision was correct. My only regret is that our team ever went to the tournament. I can assure you that it would not have gone if I had any idea that integrated teams would be there. I am a Mississippian, and I believe in what the people of the state stand for. I will not, in my official actions, deviate from long-established policies and cherished traditions." An alum of the class of 1950 sent a telegram expressing his "extreme disgust and embarrassment" at the call to bring the team home. Hilbun's response: "I am extremely sorry that my decision caused you embarrassment; however, my embarrassment would have been much greater than yours if I had acted otherwise."[4]

Against this backdrop, and with this president still calling the shots, the Maroons hoped that a 1959 SEC title would mean a NCAA tournament berth.

State still had to actually win the league crown to force Hilbun's hand. On Valentine's Day, five days after the epic win over Kentucky, State traveled to Gainesville, Florida, and had no problem with Florida, winning 105–68. Howell scored 43 to break the record for most points scored in the Gators' gym, but not without some prodding. McCarthy substituted for him with five minutes to play and his points total sitting at 41. But when the crowd chanted, "We want Howell," McCarthy obliged, and Howell made two free throws to reach his final total.

Bailey Howell dunking the ball in a Mississippi State practice. Notice the skylights in the gymnasium roof. *Courtesy of University Archives, Mississippi State University Libraries.*

Two days later at Georgia, State improved to 11-1 in league play with a 76–56 win over the Bulldogs. By now, State had risen to no. 5 in the Associated Press poll and no. 7 in the UPI listing. The only thing standing in front of State clinching a NCAA tournament invitation was its annual swing through the Louisiana schools, during which it would first play LSU and then Tulane. It would have little problem with either team. The Maroons dispatched the Tigers, 75–67, on a Saturday night in which the Baton Rouge fans shot at State players with BB guns. Two nights later in New Orleans, Mississippi State clinched its first Southeastern Conference championship by beating the Green Wave, 65–51. But the conversation about whether that would lead to a first-ever NCAA tournament berth, which started in earnest after the Maroons had beaten Rupp and Kentucky, had yet to produce any solution.

It was undoubtedly a statewide conversation, often finding its way onto the front pages and the editorial pages of the state's major newspapers. For some three weeks in the late winter of 1959, it was the state's hot story. Instead of Babe McCarthy and Bailey Howell grabbing the publicity surrounding the Maroons' basketball teams, the quotes were often coming from houses of political decision in Jackson.

The state's ultimate policymaking board for higher education was the board of trustees of the state's Institutions of Higher Learning, a body formed in 1944 to govern the state's four-year colleges. Unlike in many states, where governance from higher education is institution-specific, with separate boards for different schools or groups of schools, Mississippi governed its nine colleges with a centralized group of trustees. In 1959, R.D. Morrow was its chairman and S.R. Evans chaired its athletic committee.

The scoreboard at State's gym may well have still been on following the win over Kentucky when the *Jackson Daily News* asked Evans what he thought about the team's chances to play in the NCAA tournament. "I'd hate to have to make up my mind if it were offered," he said. "It is all according to the circumstances. We would have to know who was playing, among other things. If the attitude of the people was against it, we couldn't very well expect it." Evans's fence-sitting would prove to be common of Mississippi politicians struggling to strike the balance between protecting segregation and respecting the sports fans of one of its largest institutions.

Russell Fox, a state representative from Claiborne County, didn't sit on the fence. "You can compromise method and manner, but you cannot compromise basic principles without sacrificing the major issue involved. I'm against the team going," he said. Governor J.P. Coleman, a native of Ackerman, some twenty-five miles west of Starkville, apparently washed his hands of the situation.

The state's major newspapers in Jackson editorialized against going to the tournament. On February 18, the *Daily News*, with James Ward as its editor, penned a fire-breathing editorial that characterized basketball as a sacrifice that would be too minor to make in the overall goal of preserving segregation:

> *Agitators are already at work creating an issue which places the entire state in an uncomfortable position of being asked, once again, to reiterate its stand on segregation. This situation isn't raised by thinking citizens but those emotionally aroused by the beat of athletic passion goaded by clapping hands and the muffled yells from hoarse-throated, rabid fans basking in the exuberance of momentary glory...The issue is: Will Mississippi forsake long-established, well-considered policy for the sake of an empty promise of another swallow of shallow bouncing, round ball glory?....Suppose for the sake of national publicity for State's team a new policy is adopted. Will this new policy be misconstrued to the nation? Will the search for and excitement of gravel-voiced applause be worth sending an invitation to the racial agitators to come on down, that Mississippi is cracking?...The Mississippi State integrated tournament issue should be settled quickly and quietly. If honored with an invitation to play in the NCAA play, simply send a wire of regrets stating the ball team and the students are all busy studying for spring exams.*

The *Clarion-Ledger* reserved its opinion for the news section. When Mississippi State students voted to play in the tournament, it appeared in the *C-L* under an all-caps headline: "THEIR OPINION." A day later, the *C-L* diced apart the 973–162 vote in favor of going to the tournament with another striking headline: "MISSISSIPPI STATE STUDENT VOTE COULD BE MISLEADING." Why? The paper said that while 1,132 voted, the school's enrollment is 4,333. That's just 25 percent turnout.

Greenville's *Delta Democrat-Times*, under the leadership of Pulitzer Prize–winning editor Hodding Carter, took a different approach. On February 22, four days after Ward's editorial in Jackson, the paper editorialized in favor of going to the tournament:

> *We believe State can win this title if the people of Mississippi get behind them the way their own student body has. For one thing, luck is running our way...Let's face it. The Maroons playing in this tournament will not affect Mississippi's stand on integration of its classrooms one way or the other...We believe most Mississippians would like to see the Maroons get their well-deserved chance at the national title. If they don't it will be the fault of a few half-baked politicians and writers who think so poorly of*

the hard-working Maroon athletes that they describe their spending 1959 record as "shallow, bouncing round ball glory."

McCarthy's words were measured, but it was clear he wanted to play. "We are only four games away from the national championship," he said after the Maroons clinched the SEC title with the win at Tulane. "Would love to get a chance to play those games."

Shortly after the Kentucky win, speculation began that McCarthy might attempt to capitalize on his newfound fame and leave Starkville. The coach confirmed that he had been contacted by Texas, which was looking to replace Marshall Hughes. Lee Baker, the sports editor of the *Daily News*, wrote an entire column on the speculation on February 13. Baker noted that Texas would be a good opportunity and that "no longer would he face such a problem as might hamstring his current Maroons' chance for post-season NCAA play for segregation is no issue for Texas teams." McCarthy's cozy relationship with the small corps of press that covered his teams suggests that he may not have minded—and may have encouraged—the talk to better his and his team's self-interest.

Regardless of motivation, McCarthy didn't pack up his young family and head off to Austin. One day before the season finale at Ole Miss, State announced that McCarthy had signed a new four-year contract. In doing so, McCarthy said all the right things. His statement from the contract announcement was as follows:

I appreciate the support of the team, the student body, the officials, and the people of Mississippi. In return for all the support which has been given us, and because I stand for the same things Mississippians have always stood for, I am happy to make my stand alongside the people of Mississippi and continue giving them at Mississippi State University the kind of basketball they like to see played. These times demand institutional and state loyalty. As a United people, we can go forward to a great Mississippi State University and a better Mississippi. I want to play my part in that march forward.

Hilbun's decision seemed a foregone conclusion. Yet with the story residing on the front pages, alumni and others deluged Hilbun's office in an attempt to ensure that they were in his ear.

A letter from Meridian contained newspaper clippings that described a recent rape of a white woman by a black man: "I am sure you feel as all of us do, that we just can't subject our young girls and other women folk to the mercies of these fiends, and to integrate in any way is just leading to the ultimate end." It was anonymously signed. A state representative from Yazoo County dismissed the overwhelming student vote in favor of going. "As for the students voting that is a minor matter because most of them are still immature and still need instruction and guidance from the wiser and older people," he wrote. A Columbus man agreed: "But then realizing that these same students, if given the opportunity, would probably vote to completely disband all classes, I am lead [sic] to believe that this opinion poll can and should be completely disregarded." More letters encouraging Hilbun to keep the team at home—or applauding his decision to do just that, which the *Daily News* reported citing anonymous sources on February 25—came from state representatives in Hinds and Wilkinson Counties, the district president of the alumni association in Jackson, the Leake County alumni association, the Marion County Board of Education, a handful of local citizens councils and even the women's auxiliary of the Citizens Council in the small Delta village of Louise.[5]

Robert B. Patterson's February 24 letter to Hilbun was a bit more significant. Patterson was the leader of the Citizens Council of America, a staunch supporter of segregation. On CCA letterhead, he penned this:

> *The Executive Committee of this Association has directed me to express their appreciation for the stand that you have taken, in the face of great pressure, in preserving the avowed principles of the taxpayers of this state…Enemies of the South have contended that Southerners believe in their principles only so long as it is expedient to do so. As a leader among Southern states, it would be tragic for Mississippi State to place her athletes on an equal footing with Negro athletes playing on an integrated team. It is a short step from playing against an integrated team to having a Negro playing on a Mississippi team. It is the natural sequence. If this Association can help in any way, please call on us.*

Hilbun responded with a modified version of the form letter he had been sending to everyone who wrote. In this one, he told Patterson, "I am sure that my decision pleased you all, for which I am grateful."[6]

It did not please everyone. Jerry Clower, the Mississippi State alum and noted country comedian, told Hilbun that he thought "a majority of our people are saying let them go." He told him that he would stand with his decision and suggested that he read James 1:5, which reads, "If any of you lack wisdom, let him ask of God, that giveth to all men liberally, and upbraideth not; and it shall be given him."

Nine signatures came on a letter from a Memphis postmark supporting participation. A 1932 graduate from Galveston, Texas, urged Hilbun "to yield to the will of the student body rather than aggravate a bad situation by penalizing youth with the prejudices of older generations."[7] Alumni chapters from Lawrence, Lee, Scott and Marion Counties, as well as Houston, Texas, wrote in favor of going. A Jackson businessman telegrammed to say that he had surveyed 171 of his customers in the southern and central parts of the state and that 159 of them supported the team playing in the tournament. Also, 23 people from Calhoun City were in favor.[8]

Hilbun tallied the results: 147 were against tournament participation, and 128 wrote in favor of it. Of the 147 in favor of staying home, 7 came from outside Mississippi. Of the 128 in favor of playing in the tournament, 39 came from outside Mississippi.[9]

The Maroons still had one game to play, though. At 12-1 in the Southeastern Conference, State had clinched the NCAA tournament invitation because it could do no worse than finish in a tie with Kentucky, over which it owned the tiebreaker. But if the Maroons wanted to win a title outright, they would need to win their season finale, set for the final day of February at rival Ole Miss.

State had already whipped the hated Rebels by twenty-nine points in Starkville on January 17. Country Graham, the Ole Miss coach, knew that his only hope was in a slow-down game to match the kind of slow-down that McCarthy was known to implement from time to time. Graham's Rebels might lose, sure. But he was probably certain of a loss if he played them conventionally. Matching styles molasses for molasses was the plan.

Howell recalled:

> We jumped off to lead on them, you know, so they had to force the action. We were playing a zone, we played a zone mostly, if we got in trouble, we'd come off our zone and play man to man. Which, I guess we were a pretty good man-to-man team, but we probably had a better zone. Well, Ole Miss froze the ball, basically, for the rest of the game, until about eight or ten minutes to go. And they had to force the action, so they'd stand out there at half court with it. The official would count off however many seconds he had to count off. And then he'd say [motions his hands forward], which meant they had to attack, they had to, they'd dribble up to the zone and turn around and throw it back out. They'd stand there, and the official would count off again. And that happened until way over late in the game....So then Ole Miss started trying to score. If they failed to score, we got the rebound [and] they fouled

In this undated photo of a student dance at Ole Miss's old gymnasium, notice the tight quarters. *Courtesy of Ole Miss Athletics.*

> *us. We'd only get one shot, one foul shot. So we went down; we missed it. So Babe said foul 'em back. We'd foul them; they'd make their foul shot. All of the sudden, whatever lead we had, it got real tight, two or three points. We were on the line again, and we shot and missed it. This is like the third or fourth time that they'd fouled. And I think I tipped in the rebound, gave us a little breathing room. We won 23–16.*

"I just talked," said Jack Cristil, the team's radio voice. "Sure was an easy game to work, I know that."

The victorious Maroons took McCarthy to the dressing room on their shoulders. Mississippi State had just finished a regular season that easily was the best in program history and would be the best in many programs' histories—24-1, with a 13-1 record in the Southeastern Conference. Mississippi State had won thirteen games in a row. It had one of the best players in the nation, if not *the* best player in the nation, in Bailey Howell. The next Associated Press poll noted that State was the fourth-best team in the nation, surely a contender for a national championship should it be able to go. Shortly after the jubilant scene in Oxford, Hilbun made his decision public:

> *Under long-standing policies and customs of the state of Mississippi, athletic teams of institutions of higher learning have not engaged in competition with integrated teams or participated in tournaments in which integrated teams were entered. This policy so far as I know has not been discarded or revised. Therefore the basketball team of Mississippi State University will not compete in the NCAA tournament this year.*

Undoubtedly, the compliant McCarthy quoted in the contract extension news release a day earlier had been made aware of the decision—if he even thought there was one to be made. In Oxford, McCarthy said that he agreed with the decision. "We'll stay home and tell everybody we're the best," McCarthy said. Back in Starkville, the news was not as well received. State students booed when hearing it and hung Hilbun in effigy. A day later, McCarthy conceded a bit. "I naturally would have liked to have taken the team to the tournament, but I won't squawk," he said. "I'll do whatever I can for the school." Howell also sounded a compliant tone. "We would like to have gone, but we made up our minds and winning the title was a great thing to us," he said. Jimmy Ward editorialized in favor of the decision in the *Daily News*, and Carl Walters took up for Hilbun in the *Clarion-Ledger*. Even the Mississippi Daughters of the American Revolution, at its annual state conference, applauded Hilbun's move.

To paint the Maroons as devastated isn't exactly accurate. Hilbun's decision was expected; an opposite decision would have probably evoked more surprise than jubilation. And in terms of goals, the NCAA tournament wasn't as big of a deal as it is today, back in the era before the wall-to-wall television coverage and the buzzer beaters that became part of every young basketball player's upbringing. To many, the National Invitation Tournament remained a more prestigious tournament, or at least as prestigious.

Yet State's acceptance of Hilbun's decision was based largely on the norms of a different era. If the leadership said it was the right decision, the students were much more willing to think that, too. "It wasn't a big part of our conversation," Howell recalled years later. "We really were focused in on just trying to win the SEC. It was just a big disappointment, but Babe said [there's] probably going to be a lot of national media in here, [and] they're going to be trying to talk to y'all; just don't say anything to anybody. We did sort of what we were told...Back then, you did what you were told."

Chapter 4

RELOADING, THEN RETURNING TO THE TOP

In the balcony of First Baptist Church in Brookhaven, Mississippi, one late winter Sunday morning in 1959, Bobby Shows and the rest of his teenage buddies were halfheartedly awaiting the start of the morning service. Below them, in the main part of the sanctuary, heads turned. Babe McCarthy, the head coach of the Southeastern Conference champion Mississippi State basketball team, was walking down the aisle. So was Jerry Simmons, his chief assistant. They chose seats in the front pew.

Shows, a tall forward for Brookhaven High's basketball team, knew right then and there where he would play college basketball. "It was about as clear as a bright light in your eyes," Shows said. "I was going right then."

Such was the way Babe McCarthy recruited. He wasn't content to send a letter or two, make the requisite phone call or appearance and then go home. He was a hustler, no doubt a significant facet to his rich personality. "He was a salesman," said Bailey Howell, whose recruitment in 1955 wasn't long after McCarthy left the petroleum sales business. "Salesmen have to be positive. Salesmen have to be able to read people." McCarthy often enlisted the help of his family. One of the earliest memories of his son, Jim, who was about five years old then, was helping to recruit Howell. "An old country road, and there's this big lanky kid coming. It's almost like a dream," he said years later. "Coach McCarthy," Doug Hutton said, "could sell an Eskimo a refrigerator."

He faced a big test of those abilities in the spring of 1959. While Bailey Howell and company had made it easy for him on the floor, they hadn't paved the way to immediate future success. Howell, Ted Usher, Kermit Davis and

Jerry Keeton were seniors that year, meaning that McCarthy and Simmons had work to do to keep up what they had started. Whether Mississippi State was to be a flash in the pan, a one-year-wonder made solely on the back of Howell, or if it were truly to become a dynasty of the caliber to challenge Kentucky, it would be the result of McCarthy's recruiting.

McCarthy had seen Shows before he walked into church that Sunday. When Shows was an undergrad at Mars Hill High, McCarthy traveled to Starkville for a hog judging contest. Shows was already six feet, four inches tall, so his ag teacher thought it worthwhile to take him over to the gym to meet McCarthy. A few years later, after transferring to Brookhaven, Shows became a coveted high school player—hence the appearance of McCarthy and Simmons at church that morning.

After the benediction, McCarthy and Simmons lunched with the Shows family. Shows was ready to sign his scholarship, but the phone rang. It was a coach from Ole Miss who had heard that McCarthy and Simmons had visited church that morning. Shows wasn't interested, though, and McCarthy left Brookhaven with a signed set of scholarship papers.

Not every player who signed with McCarthy in that offseason came so clear-cut. Take Leland Mitchell. One of ten children of a carpenter on Mississippi's Gulf Coast, Mitchell had to fight and claw his way to the top. He was on a boxing team in school and went to work at a shrimp place after finishing the eighth grade. "I was fourteen, but I was tall, told them I was sixteen," Mitchell said. A year later, he was tending bar at a fish camp. "I could make any drink you can name," he said. And by his senior year, he was working painting radio towers.

Yet Mitchell remained in school and began to develop quite the reputation as a basketball player—so much so that by the time he was a senior, he was playing on full scholarship at Pearl River Junior College and had made the all-state team to boot. That next summer, he visited a brother who was a part owner of a traveling carnival in the Midwest, worked for him for a while and then went to Dallas to visit another brother, who just happened to know the coaching staff at the University of Texas. Upon arriving in Austin, Mitchell was told that the Longhorns didn't need another forward. Still, he stuck around long enough to play some pickup games and more than hold his own. The Texas coach offered a one-year scholarship, but Mitchell declined. He wanted a full four-year guarantee. Using connections from back home, he got in touch with McCarthy, who also only offered a one-year scholarship. But since it was home, and since State had just completed that successful season, Mitchell accepted.

Tall Leland Mitchell drives to the hoop. *Courtesy of Mississippi State University Athletics.*

Shows remembered Mitchell's arrival differently. He wasn't even sure that McCarthy knew that Mitchell was coming to Starkville until he actually arrived. He recalled being in Starkville shortly before classes started in the fall of '59 and McCarthy asking Shows's father to take Mitchell to Starkville High School's gym for an evaluation. He and Shows played one-on-one; Shows's father reported back to McCarthy that he was worth at least a one-year scholarship, maybe four.

W.D. Stroud grew up in Forest, Mississippi, the son of a farmer. He had an obvious nickname, "Red," the color of his curly, full head of hair. When he arrived on campus, McCarthy first wanted to know if he played guard or forward. "Nah," Stroud was said to have responded. "I'm a shooter." But Jack Berkshire, for one, wasn't immediately impressed. "When we first finally went over, I was looking around for Red Stroud," he recalled. "When I saw him, he was not very heavy at all. He was very slim and didn't look strong at all. I don't see how he can be what they're talking about. But right away, it was evident that he was an outstanding shooter and had a chance to be a really good offensive player."

Joe Dan Gold weaves through defenders to get to the basket. *Courtesy of Mississippi State University Athletics.*

Joe Dan Gold hailed from Benton, Kentucky, a small town of a few thousand in the westernmost portion of that basketball-mad state. He was the youngster of the group. Born on June 7, 1942, Gold was barely seventeen years old when he arrived for his freshman year at Mississippi State. Though teammates would come to love his toughness, hard work and other intangible qualities, he brought with him a most eye-opening skill: his jump shot was the flattest anyone had ever seen. As the story goes, Gold's junior high school gymnasium had an abnormally low roof. In order for Gold to shoot, he had to learn to fire line drives.

The arrival of the freshman class in the late summer of 1959 would change an already-evolving Mississippi State basketball program forever. But NCAA rules would keep such evolution under wraps for the winter. As freshmen, they weren't eligible to play for the varsity team.

Transition at Mississippi State during the 1959–60 academic year was not limited to the basketball team. On December 30, 1959, it was announced that president Ben Hilbun would retire. That left Mississippi State searching for a new president on the verge of the challenge of integration. In Hilbun, State had what was essentially a good ol' boy: a Jones County native, a State graduate and a man who had essentially no other stops in his career beyond Starkville. To replace him, the board of trustees went in the entirely opposite direction. It chose Dean W. Colvard, the dean of the school of agriculture at North Carolina State.

Colvard, who a few months earlier had been offered the agriculture school deanship at Ohio State, didn't immediately reciprocate State's advances. He had been to Mississippi State before, about ten years earlier, "and I had not been greatly impressed," he wrote. Yet he agreed to visit the campus for an interview and returned impressed. He and his wife, Martha, added up the pros and cons of a move. Residing on the con list were the state's racial turmoil and the brewing storm clouds of integration. The sit-ins at Woolworth's in nearby Greensboro, North Carolina, were fresh on his mind. None of the colleagues he trusted advised him to accept.[10]

When the trustees interviewed Colvard, they didn't initiate the race discussion. He did. Even then, the board didn't ask for any specific attitude or philosophy on race. If they had, they might not have liked what they would have heard. "My wife and I had never considered ourselves zealous crusaders for integration, but we had on many occasions supported equal opportunities and justice for all races," he wrote. And when weighing all the negative feedback his colleagues had given him, he wrote, "I find myself not running away from the potential race problem as most people think I should. It is a major issue of our time and somehow, while I hope I do not have to be involved in it, I have difficulty in feeling that this should be cause to abandon the idea of going to Mississippi."[11]

So he accepted the job. As he drove into Mississippi west from Alabama on July 3, 1960, he took note of a billboard that read "Impeach Earl Warren," a reference to the chief justice of the United States.[12] The Supreme Court's 1954 decision in *Brown v. Board of Education* set in motion the slow, winding and often violent road of integration in southern schools.

Colvard was a southerner, though not in the Deep South sense that a Mississippian would be. According to his memoir, he was born in Ashe County, North Carolina, on July 10, 1913. He attended Virginia-Carolina High School, appropriately named for its residence on the state line. He graduated from Berea College in Kentucky in 1935, where he met his wife, the former Martha Lampkin. They married in 1939. His first job was at a junior college in Brevard, North Carolina, where he directed a student self-help program, taught agriculture courses and managed the college farm. After two years there, it was grad school at the University of Missouri, where he earned a master's in animal physiology. He returned to his home state to take over as superintendent of an agricultural research station, which was taken over by the army after Japan bombed Pearl Harbor. Colvard then had to locate and spearhead two new research stations. After the war, he earned another graduate degree, this time from Purdue University, where he also earned his PhD. He started a long career at N.C. State, first as professor and head of the department of animal industry. In 1953, he was named the dean of the school of agriculture.

Mississippi State's 1959–60 basketball season started with the kind of promise that usually surrounds a team coming off a historic season such as the one the Maroons had just ended. But it didn't take a long look at State's roster to realize that a 24-1 record, a top-five national ranking and a conference championship wouldn't be coming. Forwards Charles Hull and Jerry Graves and guard John Hutchison were the team's only returning lettermen.

On opening night, December 2, 1959, Mississippi State retired Howell's jersey. The Maroons won 66–50 over Troy State in front of 4,000. After a 3-0 start, State's winning streak was snapped on December 9 against Louisiana Tech in front of 2,800 at Jackson's City Auditorium. State took a 49–47 lead on Hull's jumper with ten minutes to play, but it was all Tech after that.

There was little to celebrate the rest of the way. The darling of the Sugar Bowl tournament a year earlier, State slinked out of New Orleans this time with an 11-point loss to Western Kentucky and a 21-point loss to Virginia Tech. The losses continued to pile up in Southeastern Conference play. State lost by 22 to Georgia Tech, by 7 to archrival Ole Miss and by 10 at Tennessee, a game that saw the Maroons score just 38 points. And in the rematch of the game of the year of 1959, State was thumped 90–59 by Kentucky in Lexington on February 8. The jubilation of a 24-1 record in 1959 turned into despair over a 12-13 record in 1960, State's first losing record since McCarthy's first year.

But on that opening night during which State retired Howell's jersey, there was a footnote in the *Clarion-Ledger*'s account: "In a preliminary game, the Mississippi State freshmen rolled over East Mississippi Junior College of Scooba, 106–39." That would prove to be a common theme. With Gold, Mitchell, Shows and Stroud leading the way, Mississippi State's freshmen wouldn't just win every game they played. They would annihilate every opponent they faced. "We were like a hand in a glove," Shows said. "We knew each other. It didn't take us long to know what each other could do, and it showed on the court."

Soon, word spread about just how good the freshmen were. "We kind of rallied all over the state, because everybody wanted to see the freshmen team play," said Jimmy Wise, who would become the team's manager. "When we played at home, it would be packed for the freshman game." Young Larry Templeton, who would go on to become the school's athletic director but who grew up on campus as the son of the campus electrical engineer, didn't miss the main event. "The freshman games were the thing, man," he said.

In the fall of 1960, Babe McCarthy knew that he had a wonderful problem on his hands—wonderful, because of just how well his band of freshmen played beside one another against other freshmen and assorted junior college teams the year earlier. McCarthy undoubtedly figured that his recruiting off the 1959 Southeastern Conference title team would be solid, but it wasn't until they played together the next year that he could see how they meshed as a team. And did they ever.

But it was a problem, too. His 1959–60 team lost more than it won, sure, but that doesn't mean it was filled with bad players. Jerry Graves, a six-foot-six post player, made the Associated Press's and coaches' All–Southeastern Conference teams, albeit on the second unit, off that so-so squad. Graves averaged a double-double that year, scoring 18.6 points per game and grabbing 10.4 rebounds per game. In a December game against Southeastern Louisiana, he grabbed a whopping 23 rebounds. Graves had the good fortune of making the free-throw line almost as often as Howell did in the seasons that preceded him. And when he got there, he was fairly consistent, making 80 percent of his free throws that year.

Graves followed the small-town mold that many of McCarthy's players fit. He grew up in Lexington, Tennessee, a town of a few thousand some three hours north of Starkville, the son of hardworking farmers. But he wasn't much of a basketball star until he hit a growth spurt in time for his sophomore season. Afterward, he became a scoring machine. The college recruiters took notice, and by his senior season, he had attracted the interest of dozens of schools. On his visits to Mississippi State, though, he was attracted to McCarthy's calm demeanor. He wanted to become a veterinarian after college, so State's veterinary program proved to be an asset. He signed with McCarthy in the spring of 1957.

Forwards Dave Glasgow, Gene Chatham, J.D. Gammel and James Edwards joined guards George Oakley and Jack Berkshire as McCarthy's experienced returnees in 1961, Graves's senior year. Berkshire was a point guard who showed no small amount of promise on the freshman team the year before, becoming its second-leading scorer. But his arrival was almost by accident. Berkshire grew up in Winfield, Iowa, a small crossroads town in the southeastern corner of the state. He played all sports but particularly loved basketball, and he especially idolized a player a few years older than him named Jim Ashmore. When Ashmore was a senior, his family moved from Winfield to Mississippi. And Ashmore continued to excel at basketball at Mississippi State, becoming the school's first all-American during the 1956–57 season. Ashmore continued to play in the National Industrial Basketball League for the Denver Truckers, and in the summer of 1958, he returned to Winfield to visit his sister. He and Berkshire reconnected, and after one particular session of one-on-one in which Berkshire acquitted himself well, Ashmore asked a question that would change his life: "Do you know where you're going to go to college?"

Berkshire didn't. He would have loved to play for the University of Iowa. When he went to visit the coach, Bucky O'Connor, he was told that there were no scholarships available, but that might change in about a month. A week later, O'Connor was killed in a car accident. Berkshire kept the Iowa idea open, but it was likely that by the end of the summer, he was going to have to choose between Northeast Missouri State, Parsons College, Iowa Wesleyan and Northern Iowa. So he told Ashmore that he hadn't made up his mind. Ashmore thought that his skills would fit in well at Mississippi State, not to mention that he knew McCarthy's team would have an opening for guards by the time Berkshire had finished his freshman season. "Would you be interested in going south?" Ashmore asked.

They called McCarthy, who said he was filled with guards in his signing class, but if he came to Starkville and could prove his worth, McCarthy could waive his out-of-state tuition and let him eat at the training table during the season. Berkshire saw a chance to play major college basketball and felt he could trust Ashmore, so his family drove him to Chicago, where he boarded the City of New Orleans train. He had never been south of St. Louis. When he walked off the train in Winona, Mississippi, the stop nearest Mississippi State, two managers picked him up. When they walked into a diner to eat, Berkshire saw for the first time the signs noting where "Colored" and "White" patrons should sit.

In his first week, Berkshire was uneasy. He was an Iowan living in the Deep South and knew nobody. To make matters worse, the offer from McCarthy was for meals at the training table only during the season, which meant that upon his arrival, he was eating his meals alone at the cafeteria. Homesick, Berkshire went to McCarthy during the first week and asked for help returning home. It wasn't going to work out, he thought. McCarthy put up little resistance and noted that the next train would leave Winona in the morning. But since there was time between now and then, why not get the rest of the freshmen together for a workout? Berkshire played well. "The next thing I knew, he talked to me and said, 'I'll tell you what: I can start your meals right now.'" Berkshire stayed, got to know his teammates and felt more at home. Later in the semester, Ashmore stopped by campus to play pickup. Ashmore picked Berkshire for his team, and the youngster again played well in front of McCarthy—so well, in fact, that McCarthy offered him a full scholarship. Berkshire never again thought about going back to Winona to catch that train.

Jack Berkshire wasn't part of McCarthy's problem. After the deft touch Berkshire had shown as a sophomore and the lack of a true heir coming up in the freshman class, the point guard position wasn't up for grabs. Neither was Jerry Graves's territory on the block. Both were team captains, after all. But the rest of the lineup remained to be determined. When State opened its season with a 77–55 win over Southeastern Louisiana in front of about four thousand on December 3, McCarthy went with a strict platoon system. The four sophomores joined junior forward Gene Chatham in the second unit. McCarthy continued to tinker throughout December, a luxury his characteristically mild early season schedule allowed. During that month, his team racked up a 56-point win over Union, the Southern Baptist college a few hours away in Jackson, Tennessee; a 31-point win over Louisiana College; a 23-point win over Spring Hill; and a 39-point win over Delta State. In Houston for a holiday tournament a few days after Christmas, the Bulldogs grabbed an 8-point win over Rice and fell by 11 to Texas. Loyola of New Orleans and Louisiana Tech also felled McCarthy's platooning Maroons. Entering Southeastern Conference play, State was a respectable 7-3.

Just as in 1959, the task of opening SEC play fell on a road trip to Auburn, which continued its excellence under Coach Joel Eaves. In 1960, Eaves's Tigers won the SEC and set a national record for field goal shooting percentage at 52.1 percent.[13] Not since 1958 had one of McCarthy's teams beaten Auburn, not even that 24-1 team from Howell's senior season—its only loss was by a whopping thirty-one points in the SEC opener at Auburn's Sports Arena.

Yet the team McCarthy would send out that night on the Plains wasn't much like the one he had used in the previous ten games. He had settled on his rotation, and as expected, the sensational freshmen of the earlier year would be used quite a bit. In addition to Graves at center and Berkshire at point guard, McCarthy started three sophomores: Leland Mitchell and Joe Dan Gold at forwards and Red Stroud at guard. It was a perfect balance. Berkshire's experience and wile would lead the team, and Graves's experience and toughness would anchor it in the post. That would help free Stroud to shoot from the wing, and the Mitchell/Gold combination combined with Graves made State formidable in the paint. Bobby Shows could come off the bench, as could veterans Dave Glasgow and Gene Chatham.

Whatever misgivings the displaced players may have had about McCarthy's roster maneuvers were probably soothed, if not otherwise snuffed out, on the night of January 7 in Auburn. State jumped ahead early, went into slowdown, made all but one of its twenty-five free throw attempts and beat the Tigers,

56–48. It was Auburn's first defeat in its home arena since 1958. As the team walked back to its hotel rooms following its pregame meal, one of the coaches nodded at the swimming pool and said they'd both jump in if the team defeated Auburn. In frigid weather late in the night of their return from the Sports Arena, McCarthy and Simmons jumped in, still in their suits and ties.

It did not take long for the win to reverberate. In Monday's *Clarion-Ledger*, Carl Walters called the team a "gen-u-win" dark horse candidate for the league title. The next few results emboldened that claim. State backed up the Auburn win with a seventeen-point win at Alabama two nights later, then dispatched Vanderbilt, thought to be a tough out, by nine. Georgia Tech, another annual contender, gave State a tough fight on January 16, but the Maroons prevailed by one in overtime thanks to Graves's stellar performance in the bonus period. "There isn't a player in basketball with more guts than Graves, especially when he walked to that free-throw line under pressure," McCarthy said afterward. State blew out Ole Miss by twenty-three, dispatched Delta State in the teams' second nonconference meeting of the year by twenty-two and then breezed past LSU (by sixteen) and Tulane (by fourteen) to open Southeastern Conference play 7-0 and set the stage for yet another hyped early February weekend that saw visits from Tennessee and Kentucky. For the second time in three years, the probable SEC title would be on the line when Adolph Rupp visited Mississippi State.

On the night of January 14, when Jerry Graves made twenty-one free throws to lead State to that nine-point win over Vanderbilt, a fan held up a sign that read, "Ding-Dong dammit!"

It was another sign of an increasing amount of tension between Mississippi State and the dean of Southern college basketball, Kentucky coach Adolph Rupp. It was believed that Rupp had gotten the Southeastern Conference to ban cowbells—so by the time he was to have entered the gym the day before Valentine's Day in 1961, that ear-splitting noise he heard in 1959 would not nearly be so offensive. (Whether Rupp led this effort is unknown; State fans to modern day continue to be on high alert when their cowbell is threatened.) A quote that appeared in the February 12 *Clarion-Ledger* that was attributed to an issue of *Sports Illustrated* did not help matters: "Hell, we could do well in the conference if we warmed up against a bunch of teachers' colleges. We can't go around playing a bunch of patsies like Mississippi State does."[14]

It would have been entirely like McCarthy to be congenial with Rupp in private but not mind the perception of a feud in public. Jimmy Wise, a team manager from that era who was probably as close to McCarthy as

Kentucky coach Adolph Rupp stands with Wildcat Johnny Cox. *Courtesy of Special Collections, University of Kentucky libraries.*

anyone, said that the two were actually close: "I think Adolph respected what Babe was able to do with mainly Mississippi kids and compete against the big boys." Laverne McCarthy, Babe's widow, recalled them being friendly. "They were okay behind the scenes," she said. "But Rupp hated to play there at Mississippi State, with the cowbells."

On Saturday night, two nights before the Kentucky showdown, Mississippi State improved to 8-0 by beating Tennessee, 72–67. Rupp's Wildcats were not as fortunate. Even though they beat Ole Miss in Jackson, they were but 5-4 and not particularly in contention for the league title—an oddity for a program so accustomed to such lofty heights. When they came to Starkville, though, they appeared nothing like a fledgling, barely .500 team. Kentucky pounced quickly, put the throttle down early in the second half and overcame a 27-point night from Graves to escape dreaded Starkville with a 68–62 win. With an estimated crowd of six thousand—some 20 percent larger than the gym's listed capacity—cheering on State, the Maroons simply could not get many shots to fall.

The Mississippi State/Rupp feud reached perhaps its most colorful—and certainly its most odorous—moment that night when someone placed a dead skunk under the Wildcats' bench. This, of course, quickly gained Rupp's attention. The whole episode, along with State students throwing paper cups onto the floor when they didn't like foul calls against their classmates, drew Rupp's pointed ire. "The throwing of paper cups was uncalled for," Rupp said, "and I sure as hell would like to know who put that damn dead skunk under our bench." If Kentucky students ever were to do something like that, "I hope we give up basketball," Rupp said, and there may not be any stronger conviction in the Bluegrass State than a statement like that.

State's first defeat in Southeastern Conference play would not have been a disaster if it were its only one. But it was not. Five days after that home loss to Kentucky, the Bulldogs were upset on the road at Florida, 59–57. After leading late, Graves was whistled for a foul for elbowing George Jung while jostling for a rebound. Jung tied the game with his two free throws. After a subsequent Florida miss, State held the ball until about ten seconds. Berkshire dribbled right but never got a chance to take the game-winning shot. Bobby Shiver stole the ball and passed it to Cliff Luyk, who nailed a jumper at the free-throw line with four seconds to play.

When Mississippi State arrived to play at Georgia two days later, it found a more curious obstacle to overcome than just the two-game losing streak that made its lead in the conference standings tenuous. A rainstorm had caused the roof of Georgia's Woodruff Hall to leak, and the game was played with towels down on the floor. Yet State went full-throttle and pummeled Georgia, 99–77, behind Graves's 34 points. It snapped the two-game losing streak and improved State to 9-2 in the conference.

If the Bulldogs could win one of their next three games—on the road at LSU, Tulane and Ole Miss—they would win at least a share of their second SEC title in three years under McCarthy. If they could win two, they would clinch the outright title…and ensure there would be yet another statewide debate about whether the team could represent the league in the NCAA tournament. Or, as *Daily News* sports editor Lee Baker put it, "Mississippi State's biennial problem has cropped up again."

Five thousand people filed into the Parker Agricultural Coliseum in Baton Rouge on February 25 to watch their so-so LSU Tigers take on the top team in the conference. They were rewarded with a hotly contested game. LSU led by 13 in the first seven minutes, but State closed that gap to a 50–50 tie with a little over ten minutes to play. The key break came with eleven seconds remaining. That's when Mitchell and George Nattin tied for possession, forcing a jump ball. Mitchell won the tip, pushing the ball out to Berkshire. He passed to Graves, who had a three-on-two in the center, with Stroud on his left and Mitchell on his right. Graves passed to Mitchell on the baseline. He knocked down the fifteen-footer, and State left with a 56–54 win.

All State needed was to beat Tulane in New Orleans and it could reenact that euphoric 1959 scene—the return from the Big Easy with another SEC title in tow. The Green Wave would not cooperate easily. Tulane raced out to a 12-point lead early in the second half, and Mitchell fouled out with just 5 points. But McCarthy had Gold and Graves, who scored 22 combined in the second half as State employed the rare pressure defense and notched a 62–57 win.

Governor Ross Barnett wired the team with his congratulations but without his permission for it to go to the tournament. The idea that the 1961 team would advance to the NCAA when the 1959 team did not was so far-fetched that the movement to send the team hardly received any traction. It took until March 1, two days after the Tulane win, for the *Clarion-Ledger* to devote much space to it. In a UPI story on the topic, Barnett said that integrated sporting contests might lead to integration across the board, so he opposed the NCAA tournament trip. Asked Barnett, "If there were a half dozen Negroes on the team, where are they going to eat? Are they going to want to go to the dance later and want to dance with our girls?"

McCarthy was typically diplomatic, saying that there hadn't been talk on the team of going and that he thinks the players "understand the situation." And his thoughts? "My wishes couldn't possibly make any difference." One reporter asked why McCarthy didn't take the team on his own, policy be damned. "I like my job," he said. In defense of his program, he referenced his recruiting coups after the 1959 team stayed at home and said that if he encounters a player on the recruiting trail for whom the NCAA tournament is important, he ends the recruitment. "There's no use wasting my time and his," he said. Said Mitchell, "I don't find anything wrong with them," in reference to black players. "I played baseball and basketball with them in Texas. But if I thought it might encourage them to want to come to our school, I wouldn't want to go." And Stroud? "Some of the boys don't like it," he said, "but they don't say much."

Team photo of the 1960–61 Southeastern Conference champions. *Courtesy of University Archives, Mississippi State University Libraries.*

So State had won the Southeastern Conference and knew that it would not be able to play in the NCAA tournament. Little wonder, then, that in its last game of the season, on March 4 at Ole Miss, the team missed thirty of its first thirty-nine shots, had too small of a rally late and lost, 74–70. The loss ended State's season at 19-6 overall and 11-3 in the SEC, and it probably cost the Maroons a chance to be ranked in the final polls. McCarthy was named the league's Coach of the Year. Graves was a consensus first team all-SEC player, and for good reason. He finished with a 54 percent shooting mark from the field, averaged 21.3 points and 10.3 rebounds per game and made 80 percent of his free throws.

Kentucky represented the SEC in the NCAA tournament. The Wildcats won an opening-round game in the Mideast Region against Morehead State before falling to Ohio State, the eventual national runner-up, in the regional title game.

A couple of months after the conclusion of Mississippi State's season, news broke of a point-shaving ring orchestrated by a man in New York City that ensnared players and teams across the country. For Mississippi State, the news hit far too close to home: Jerry Graves's name was involved.

The Associated Press reported that Graves received $4,750 for shaving points in seven games. (Point shaving is when a player purposely plays poorly or otherwise attempts to influence his team to lose or win by fewer points than the gambling line in order for that player or an accomplice to make money by betting the "under.") Interviewed from his home in Lexington, Tennessee, Graves admitted to accepting the bribes but not shaving the points to earn the money. "I played my best for Coach McCarthy in every game. I never shaved points. I would just give my opinion. And I never thought we would lose. And he would bet, and if he won he'd give me some money." Graves said that Aaron Wagman, the outfit's ringleader, told him that he could make "a lot of money" if he could throw two of State's final three games. But those games were critical in winning the SEC title. "I told him no deal," he said. State won two of its final three games.

Writing in the *Clarion-Ledger*, Carl Walters pinpointed two games that he thought cast doubt on Graves's claims. Against Kentucky, State was to either lose or to win by not more than one point; it lost by six. Against Ole Miss, State was to lose by more than two points; it lost by four. (Though there was no shame in losing to a Kentucky team of that era, the Ole Miss loss stuck out. The Rebels were 10-13 before that game.)

Colvard called it a "shocking and most regrettable situation," inserting the "shocking and" part into his statement apparently at the last moment. "Now that guilt has been established," Colvard's statement read, "it is clear that Jerry Graves was the victim of too great a temptation. We feel that the greater degree of guilt is on the part of those who solicited his participation." The May 8 *Sports Illustrated*, though, was not as kind. It included Colvard's mug shot among six other university presidents and NCAA chief Walter Byers as those who "should share in the guilt for the corruption of the players who took bribes from gamblers to fix games."[15]

The roots of Babe McCarthy's SEC championship-winning style of basketball precede Graves, Howell, Davis or Keeton, and they were forged in much more humble locales than the gyms of the Southeastern Conference. Those roots can be traced all the way back to tiny Baldwyn, where that 1948 team of his won the state title...but not much before that. McCarthy did not play basketball in high school, learning the game only during his stint in the air force. Bobby Nichols, who played on McCarthy's junior high teams, recalled McCarthy studying the game, though not to the extent that it produced brain-puzzling plays. "He would set our plays up and start our plays, but they were simple plays, elementary plays," Nichols said. "Just take the ball to the basket and get it to the basket."

Coach Babe McCarthy in his later career.
Courtesy of Mississippi State University Athletics.

McCarthy's brilliance was more mental. He would not be underprepared. Before big games, he would stay up until the wee hours. "They knew every player on the team," Billy Roberson, McCarthy's assistant, recalled of McCarthy and his brother-in-law, Nelson Vandiver. "They had the other team figured out from A to Z." Yet McCarthy's mental superiority wasn't limited to the scouting report. He was a master motivator from his very first teams. "He had a God-given talent that allowed him to take basketball players that were already players that loved the game, that could play the game, and then he molded them into a player that would give him all the energy that they had," Nichols said. McCarthy told his Baldwyn charges, who were still teenagers, to play mind games. "You get a guy mad at you, smile at him," Nichols recalled McCarthy as saying. "He'll be so mad then he loses reason…and then you've got the advantage. Don't ever get mad at yourself. You control. You stay in control. You act. Don't react. Don't ever react." Those traits had been honed by the time McCarthy arrived in Starkville less than a decade later.

"He was able to pull out the best of every player," Shows said. Early in the class of 1963's time at State, Stroud, Mitchell and Shows broke one of McCarthy's rules. Shows, who related the story, doesn't remember which one, but it wasn't a major one—"came in late, caught drinking a soda pop, something." McCarthy called the trio into his office and set out to hand down discipline. He told Mitchell to start running, and he'd tell him when to stop. (Shows didn't remember what he gave Stroud.) "And then he said, 'Bobby, you stay here.' And he sent the two of them out, and I remember that was the most humiliating time in my life because Coach gave me that old 'I'm disappointed in you, I had more respect for you'—that kind of thing. He knew that would get me more than running the stands. And yet, I think he realized that talking to Leland would be like talking to a stone wall."

McCarthy was a player's coach. Berkshire had played for the exact opposite in his early years of high school—a disciplinarian who was prone to yelling until he was red in the face, a coach who was more negative than positive. McCarthy was the opposite. "Babe was just inspirational," Berkshire said. "He was an amazing guy...The players just loved playing for him. You'd have players who didn't get to play, and you'd have some of that, but he was just able to motivate people in a quiet way but a very forceful way." Mitchell likened his voice to that of longtime entertainer Art Linkletter. Gene Chatham, a backup in the early '60s, noted the ease with which McCarthy dealt with people—players, fans, administrators, anyone. "Babe could turn in either direction," Chatham said. "He could be a country guy in Baldwyn or he could talk to the most sophisticated group of people in the United States...He could be country or he could be city. He could go either way." Few remember him cursing. "He was an encourager who would pat you on the back," Howell said. "I can't remember him ever being real angry."

Recalled Wise, McCarthy's trusted manager, during the early '60s at State:

The thing that best describes Babe is, he would call a timeout in a critical game. Let's say you're trailing by one, and you've got the ball and there's twenty seconds left. He would stand there in the huddle, and he would say, "Okay, what do y'all want to do?" And we would have players who would actually say—Leland, for example, "Get it to me on the low post. I can beat my man." And [McCarthy would] say, "That's what we're going to run." Or Red would say, "Hey, set a double pick, if I get to the corner, I'm going to nail it." He'd say, "That's what we're going to do." I mean, he was a ballplayer's coach. Instead of saying, "Hey, we're going to do this and this," then he would let the players [decide]. And I think what that did, that built their confidence.

Before one particular meeting with Ole Miss, McCarthy feigned being late. He wasn't in the gym for warm-ups and wasn't in the dressing room when the Bulldogs were lacing up their shoes to run out onto the floor. "We kept waiting and waiting for him to come in and give some kind of talk about beating Ole Miss," recalled Larry Lee, a player on the early 1960s teams. "Just moments before we were about to go out on the court, he walked in, and in just a low tone of voice, he said, 'I've got four words to say: Ole Miss is here.' That was it."

"Coach McCarthy was the kind of person," recalled Doug Hutton, a guard from 1962 to 1964, "[that] no matter how bad you felt about yourself, when he talked to you you'd leave feeling good about yourself."

And yet to describe McCarthy as one who recruited well, smiled a lot and just rolled the ball onto the gym floor and let his players run is shorting him, too. Dean Smith, who won a pair of national titles as the head coach at the University of North Carolina, would long be hailed as the man who popularized the "Four Corners" offense in the 1960s. It was a style that spread the floor—four players in each corner of the half-court, with one in the middle handling the ball—and resulted in a slowdown that could help save a lead and let time run off the clock in the days before the shot clock. Yet those close to McCarthy swear that he was running it well before Smith was in Chapel Hill.

"Babe would say, 'Boys, get me three points. Get us three points. And then I'll take over,'" recalled Nichols, who played on McCarthy's junior high teams in Baldwyn in the late 1940s. "We knew what was coming about—Four Corners was coming. Of course, we didn't like Four Corners—we didn't get to shoot!" McCarthy had a different name for it: the "Domino Five." Berkshire recalled it being the catalyst to State's 1959 win over Kentucky. McCarthy called a team meeting the morning before the game. "It was typical Babe," Berkshire said.

> *We were all in the dressing room. He got the chalk, got on the board, he said, "Boys, I had a dream last night of how we can beat Kentucky." And that's how he started. He drew a Four Corners up on the wall there, on the board, [and] said, "This is what we're going to do: We're going to take Ted Usher, and Bailey's going to be down by the basket, and Ted's going to be down close to that area of the floor in one of the two corners and the other three are going to be out by half court. You're going to hold the ball until they come out to get you. Then you're going to throw it in to Ted and he's going to play two-man with Bailey." And he said as long as we're tied or we have the lead, that's what we're going to do. That was the Four Corners he drew up. And that's what beat Kentucky that game, because nobody could take Bailey one-on-one.*

The Four Corners, the stall, the Domino Five—by whatever name, it was largely disliked, even by some who benefited from all of its winning. "Aw, just terrible," said Howell, who was an all-American largely running the system in 1959. But it wasn't that Howell was selfishly disgusted with the style—he was *selflessly* disappointed. "Just think about them," he said, referring to his State teammates. "Basically, the fun part of the game is shooting, I guess, and they didn't get to shoot hardly at all." Yet in that, Howell found an endorsement for McCarthy's ability to handle people. To convince teammates to go along with such a boring style, Howell said, was a credit to McCarthy.

Mississippi State basketball under McCarthy was not a particularly fun brand to watch, except that it provided that one trademark that kept fans packing into the New Gym—winning, and in bunches. The wins, along with his easy personality, made McCarthy a statewide celebrity. When fans who missed Jack Cristil's radio broadcast would wake up the next morning and want to know the score, "They wouldn't ask, 'How'd State do last night?'" recalled Jerry Keeton, a member of the 1959 team. "They'd say, 'How'd Babe's boys do last night?' That's just the way the feeling was."

Said Cristil, "Everybody loved him. They thought Babe hung the moon. You know, we didn't have a hell of a lot to shout about at State, and that gave people something to shout about."

In a sport dominated in Mississippi by Johnny Vaught's Ole Miss Rebels, Mississippi State started its 1961 football season on an upbeat tone. The Bulldogs—as they were now more commonly referred to, as opposed to the "Maroons"—started the year with five wins and three losses. A win over Auburn on November 11 inspired at least some hope. But Coach Wade Walker's Bulldogs would play two top-ten teams to close the year—LSU and Ole Miss—and would lose both games. A thirty-point shellacking at the hands of Ole Miss sealed Walker's fate; he was soon removed as football coach and installed as athletic director.

As the late fall moved into basketball season, expectations were remarkably higher, and for good reason. Mississippi State returned four starters from the 1961 Southeastern Conference champions—Leland Mitchell, Joe Dan Gold, Red Stroud and Jack Berkshire. Jerry Graves, the lone departing senior, was statistically the team's best player. But the upside of the four juniors and Berkshire's senior leadership at point guard overshadowed the loss. Stan Brinker, a six-foot-five sophomore, would take over for Graves in the post. As was the custom for a McCarthy-coached team, State would get a few games in early December to ease into a rhythm. Down went Southeastern Louisiana, 96–73; Southwestern Louisiana, 88–61; Louisiana Tech, 81–58; Delta State, 84–55; and Louisiana College, 113–70. The Bulldogs were 5-0 before they were ever significantly tested, and those games came on December 15 and December 19 at Murray State and Memphis State, respectively. At Cutchin Fieldhouse in Murray, Kentucky, the Racers pulled to within 1 point, at 52–51, when the new guy, Brinker, made a bucket; the Bulldogs went into a slowdown that led to a 69–57 win. In front of 5,559 at Ellis Auditorium in downtown Memphis, the Tigers led early, but State, behind Mitchell's 20, led at halftime and never trailed in the second half.

Sharpshooting guard W.D. "Red" Stroud pulls down a rebound. *Courtesy of Mississippi State University Athletics.*

So here was Mississippi State, undefeated through seven games, drawing national attention owed in no small part to the 1961 SEC title, having passed a pair of respectable tests and ready for more. Those tests would come in New Orleans, just like in Howell's senior season, at the Sugar Bowl tournament. Maryland, Louisville and LSU composed the rest of the Sugar Bowl field, and each owned wins over major college teams thus far into the season. State would get Maryland's Terrapins first. In front of 4,500 at Loyola University's Field House, the two teams delivered a thriller. State found itself in foul trouble on its front line, as Brinker fouled out with 4:39 to play. The Bulldogs trailed by as many as 5 before Red Stroud went on a tear. He scored 10 of the team's final 11 points, including a twenty-footer with four seconds to play that followed a nearly minute-long stall that lifted State to a 64–62 win. Against LSU a night later, it was considerably easier. State won going away, by 22, and Stroud was named the event's most outstanding player.

Undefeated at 9-0 and the defending conference champion, Mississippi State would have appeared to be a no-brainer as the league favorite entering conference play. Yet there was Kentucky, at 10-1, with the sterling pedigree and the higher national regard—no. 3 in the Associated Press poll (State was ninth). Carl Walters of the *Clarion-Ledger* also mentioned Tulane as a candidate for the top spot in the league and wrote that "the fact that both State and Tulane meet Kentucky at Kentucky this season is a major factor in the general favoritism now being evidenced toward the Bluegrass Brigade."

Babe McCarthy took notice. "Everybody has been so durn busy talking about Cotton Nash they don't know there is another good sophomore in the Southeastern Conference," he told the *Nashville Tennessean* on the eve of his team's game at Vanderbilt. He was referring to his guard, Doug Hutton. "Hutton is one of the unsung stars of the conference. He's only 5-10. But his size fools you. He can dunk the ball. He runs the 100 in 10 flat. He had a tremendous high school and freshman record. He scored 47 points in the semifinals of the state high school tournament in the afternoon and came back that night with 54 to break his own record. Doug's got an 11-point average and he hasn't played even half of any of our games…I'd just as soon everybody keeps on talking about their sophomores and forget about mine and let us win as many as we can."

Vanderbilt would pose a formidable roadblock toward that goal. After State opened SEC play with a comeback win over Auburn at home and saw its home game against Alabama postponed due to an ice storm, it entered Vandy's Memorial Gym on January 13. Well, technically it did. Not effectively. The Bulldogs didn't make a field goal in the first six minutes of the game, finished the first half nine of thirty-two from the field and trailed by 14 at the break. The final result wasn't much prettier: Vanderbilt won, 100–86, handing Mississippi State its first defeat of the season. State shot a mere 33.7 percent from the field. McCarthy was baffled at how flat his team appeared. It was the first time in four years State allowed an opponent to score in triple digits. Beyond that, though, it made winning the SEC in back-to-back years exceedingly difficult. State conceded a game to Kentucky, which was undefeated in the league, and its chance to get one back in a head-to-head matchup rested not in the friendly din of cowbells back in Starkville. State would almost certainly have to beat Kentucky in Lexington, something it had not done since 1924.

It would also need to go undefeated, or pretty close to it, the rest of the way. At Georgia Tech two nights after the Nashville defeat, that mission seemed doomed. State again nearly went six minutes in the first half without a field goal before Stroud picked up the Bulldogs and led their fight out of their funk. Down one in the final seconds, State got a gift when a Tech player missed a layup alone under the basket and Gold got the rebound. After fumbling the ball, Mitchell picked it up, threw up the court to Hutton, who had a two-on-one with Stroud at his side. He passed to Stroud, who made a layup as the horn sounded, stunning 4,892 at Alexander Memorial Coliseum. "Well," McCarthy said, "I've always said I'd rather be lucky than rich or smart."

McCarthy provided one of his more indelible moments at that game. Protesting what he felt were too many foul calls on his team, McCarthy walked onto the playing floor to yell at the referee. The ref shot back, "Babe, for every step it takes you to get back to the bench, it's a technical [foul]." Babe froze and then looked back at the players on his bench. "Come get me, boys," he said, and the players picked him up and returned him to the sideline. McCarthy earned a technical, but just one, and even the ref couldn't help but laugh.

Something about that Atlanta trip lit a spark under the Bulldogs. Alabama, playing in Starkville two days after the Georgia Tech game as a makeup for the weather-postponed game that was supposed to have been played before State's loss to Vanderbilt, was no contest (State won, 67–40). In Oxford four days later, Hutton's second-half three-point play propelled State to a lead it wouldn't relinquish in a 61–57 win over the archrival. Stepping outside of conference, as was usual for late January, State beat Northeast Louisiana, 89–79, and then ventured to Cleveland, Mississippi, where it demolished Delta State, 106–76. At LSU on February 3, the result was much the same as it was when the two teams met in the Sugar Bowl tournament shortly after Christmas—a big State win, this time by 21. Though the road was bumpy, State recovered from that early-season hiccup at Vanderbilt to be 16-1 overall and 5-1 in the league play when it went to Tulane, one of the league's toughest teams that year, on February 5.

Coach Cliff Wells arrived at the small private university in Uptown New Orleans shortly after the conclusion of World War II and built a deceptively solid basketball program. In 1948 and 1949, his Green Wave team finished second in the conference. And for much of the early to mid-1950s, Tulane was among the league's middle-tier teams. Tulane had dropped off by 1958, when it finished ninth in the conference, but Wells had recruited well enough to give Green Wave fans a reason to think that their team was back on the upswing. Guard Jim Kerwin and forward Jack Ardon were among the best players in the conference entering the 1961–62 season, with both making the all-SEC second team a year earlier. Ardon was a staunch rebounder, but Kerwin was opening the most eyes with his scoring. He averaged 20.5 points per game in 1960–61, leading to him being named a third team all-American. He entered the Mississippi State game having just scored 41 in the Green Wave's 107-77 whipping of Ole Miss. Tulane was 9-2, its lone losses coming out of conference. In addition to Ole Miss, Tulane had beaten Florida and Georgia—a 3-0 league record that was hardly as tested as State's resume up to that point. The winner would likely be the only team that could challenge Kentucky for the 1962 conference crown.

This time, State avoided the early lull that plagued some of its previous efforts, taking the lead at the 14:20 mark of the first half and owning a 12-point halftime advantage. Leland Mitchell had one of his best nights, scoring 29 and making thirteen of his twenty-five shots. Kerwin was underwhelming—he scored 12, well below his average. The crowd of 5,600 at Tulane Gym came hoping to see their basketball fortunes revived and their conference championship dreams validated. Instead, some were throwing paper onto the floor in the final minutes of a 70–59 Mississippi State win.

Even though State had a game at Tennessee between its showdown with Adolph Rupp's Wildcats, the conversation turned to Kentucky even before the Bulldogs could exit the locker room. "I don't know if we can beat them, but we're ready," McCarthy said. "I think we're as good as Kentucky. We can run with them and we can shoot with them, but they'll be playing on their home court and it's just a question of whether we can beat them in Lexington." In grouping the upcoming Knoxville-to-Lexington road trip for his team, McCarthy called it "the biggest trip we've ever taken, and we'll be playing the two most important games we have ever played. We've got to have both of them to have a chance at the championship. Of course, we've won championships before, but we didn't win them on the road like we'll have to do now."

The Kentucky game meant more to McCarthy and State than just the 1962 SEC title. It meant revenge. One year earlier, Adolph Rupp's Wildcats came to Starkville and left with a win. When the State players moped back to the locker room afterward, there was a black wreath, with the words "Rest in Peace" inscribed on it, hanging from the door. It being no time to poke fun at the Bulldogs, still sweaty and smarting from the loss, the quick reaction was to tear it to pieces. But McCarthy sensed an opportunity. He took the wreath, carried it into his office and put it in on a shelf in his coat closet. One year later, as State was getting ready to pack for the Tennessee-Kentucky trip, McCarthy summoned Jimmy Wise, the manager. "Carry that wreath with us," he said.

There was the little matter of the Tennessee Volunteers in the way, but that would prove to be a trifling worry. State withstood the Vols' early rallies and won going away, 91–67. John Sines, the Tennessee coach, gave the shooting edge in the MSU-UK matchup to State but the defensive edge to Kentucky. "If you get a lead on them," he said, "you can take them."

In pouring-down rain in Lexington, Wise hid the funeral wreath under a raincoat and brought it into Memorial Gymnasium. It lay there during the game in a travel bag under one of Mississippi State's bench chairs.

McCarthy pulled out every motivational strategy he could find. The night before the game, McCarthy challenged each of his players to find someone to whom they would dedicate their efforts to beat Kentucky. "I want you to call them and tell them you're going to play in honor of them," McCarthy said, according to Shows. McCarthy's pregame speech focused on Joe Dan Gold, the native of the small western Kentucky hamlet of Benton, who McCarthy referred to mostly as "Joe D." Members of Gold's family had made the long drive across the state to Lexington to see him play in the basketball cathedral they knew well. Kentucky didn't have a scholarship for Gold when he came out of Benton High, though, and that's what McCarthy reminded his Bulldogs as the minutes ticked down before tipoff. "Let's get this one for Joe D.," McCarthy told his team. Then he opened the door and let them run into the crowd of more than ten thousand. "When we went out of that dressing room, you could feel it that night," Wise said.

So could Kentucky. If State's goal, at Sines's encouraging, was to take the lead early and hold it, it was accomplished. Kentucky only saw a level contest at 0–0 and 2–2. Midway through the first half, Leland Mitchell's two layups, a Gold layup and Stroud's three-point play gave State a 20–12 lead. After a Kentucky run of sorts, State stretched its halftime lead to 28–22 on buckets from Hutton, Mitchell and Stroud. "Free throws and layups," McCarthy told his team at halftime. "We're going to make them come to us." (Later, McCarthy would say this about his halftime speech: "I told my boys at the half to dribble the ball for fifteen minutes and play defense for five.") State implemented its stall in the second half, and whenever Kentucky pressed to make shots to get back into the game, State rebounded the misses and started the slow cycle all over again. Kentucky cut the lead to 3 late in the second half, but State again held. Stroud was fouled with 1:37 to play and missed his free throws, leaving an opening for the Wildcats. But the Wildcats took two bad shots, and their chances were essentially through when Stroud made a pair of free throws with thirty-four seconds to play, putting State up by 5.

In the waning moments, McCarthy motioned to Wise to get the wreath ready. Wise was confused. Surely McCarthy only wanted to take it back to the dressing room and not cause a scene in front of all those Kentucky fans, right? "We're fixing to hang it on their basket," McCarthy told Wise. Sure enough, when the final horn sounded, McCarthy led Wise to the basket, where members of the team lifted him on their shoulders, and he placed the wreath on the iron behind the cylinder. "Nobody in the stands made a move," Wise recalled years later. "They got stone silent, and they knew what it was all about." (While not casting doubt on the authenticity of the wreath a year earlier, Berkshire still chuckled at the story. "You wouldn't think Babe would make up something like that, would you, just to get us motivated?")

Wreath or no wreath, Mississippi State's win at Kentucky was monumental. On the surface alone, winning on such a formidable home floor against the nation's most storied program was impressive enough. But now, Mississippi State had the inside track to win its second straight SEC title and its third in four years. Tied in the league standings with one loss each, State controlled its destiny as it now owned the tiebreaker over the Wildcats. Five games remained for State, but unlike its previous two parades to the SEC title, all five—Florida, Georgia, LSU, Tulane and Ole Miss—would be played in Starkville. McCarthy cautioned his fans to realize that there were five games remaining before the real celebration could begin, but that didn't stop hundreds of fans from ringing their cowbells and blowing their horns in the winter night in Starkville shortly after the win. About three hundred met the team at the airport when it arrived the next day, and a crowd estimated at four thousand gathered in front of Lee Hall for an impromptu celebration. "I wish each one of you could have been there to see coach Adolph Rupp's face," Assistant Coach Jerry Simmons told the crowd. Writing in the *Clarion-Ledger*, Carl Walters called the win "one of the all-time great sports accomplishments by a Mississippi team."

It remained to be seen if it would propel the powers-that-be to make the team one of the great societal accomplishments in Mississippi history. The 1959 precedent, further reinforced by the team staying at home again in 1961, appeared solid. Butch Lambert, a state representative from the northeast Mississippi hill country, sparked some discussion in the legislature to try to change the unwritten law, but it didn't gain much traction. "Some of the lawmakers would like to see them play," he told the Associated Press, "but didn't want their vote on a resolution to go on record."

The legislature was probably the wrong place for the discussion, seeing as how one, the "unwritten law" was by definition not written, so the statehouse lacked previous policy to change; and two, legislative interference in the inner workings of a state-run university would be frowned upon by accrediting bodies. Still, Lambert hoped for a better outcome. "I'm not for playing on a regularly scheduled basis with integrated teams, but it seems foolish to pass up national honors when not playing in Mississippi and when they might not meet an integrated ball club. If it were definite [that] we knew who State would play and it was an integrated club, that would be a different matter. Is there anything wrong with five white boys winning the national championship?"

Dean W. Colvard, Mississppi State's president during the 1961, 1962 and 1963 championship runs. *Courtesy of University Archives, Mississippi State University Libraries.*

Colvard, the university president, pondered the question. He confided in his diary that in 1961 he was in favor of the team going but that the question was never posed to him. That might've been for the best, Colvard thought, because he realized that he didn't have the political capital to make such a move. But by 1962, he felt that the talk surrounding the team was intensifying. On February 23, 1962, after easy wins over Florida and Georgia brought his team ranked among the top five in the country and three games away from a SEC title, Colvard wrote this: "If it were my decision, I would let them go, but it will be far better for the pressure for change to be felt by political leaders than for me to attempt to change the longstanding custom without the help of public opinion. Many people in Mississippi are ready for a change in policy, but the predominant mood of the people still is not to play. This is likely to change before many more years."[16]

The *Reflector*, Mississippi State's student newspaper, had perhaps the most cogent observation in an editorial that came just before the season finale at

Team photo of the 1961–62 Southeastern Conference champions. *Courtesy of University Archives, Mississippi State University Libraries.*

Ole Miss, when it was all but confirmed that the team would miss the NCAA tournament for the third time if it were to beat the Rebels. "The unwritten law," the editorial noted, "grows in stature each time it becomes necessary for its enforcement." Examined in that context, the "unwritten law" became more and more peculiar. Here was a custom hardly a decade old, at least in its current form, that could have easily been overthrown by then president Ben Hilbun with the 24-1 SEC champion team in 1959 that was led by Bailey Howell. He refused to, and now, three years later, every implementation of the "unwritten law" seemed weightier than the rest—even when the current president, philosophically, was against it. The *Reflector* cited help from the most unexpected of sources, the sports editor of the newspaper at Ole Miss, the *Mississippian*. Jimmie Robertson, its editor, observed that other Deep South states didn't view such a policy as an essential plank in their platforms of segregation.

State's performance against Ole Miss on March 3 almost rendered such handwringing useless. Wins over LSU and Tulane had put State on the precipice of the SEC title, but Ole Miss, which entered 12-12, took a 37–28 halftime lead. Joe Dan Gold came to the rescue early in the second half, scoring seven straight. Hutton's long jumper with 10:50 to play put

State up 50–49. Given a stronger lead a few moments later, State went into the stall and pulled out a 63–58 win. For the second straight year and third year in four, Mississippi State was the basketball champion of the South's major schools. For the second year out of four, it finished a season with a 24-1 record and undoubted status as one of the country's best basketball teams.

McCarthy, in a public position that had evolved since his first encounter with the question in 1959, came out strongly in favor of his team being able to advance to the NCAA regional in Iowa City, Iowa. "As basketball coach, I think the boys should be allowed to play against integrated teams away from home," he said. "However, I will abide by the decision passed down by those I work for. I feel that a majority of the people of Mississippi would favor our playing against teams out of state." Just three years earlier, he had said that "these times demand institutional and state loyalty." Now, he was begrudgingly accepting a position that "those I work for" had taken.

The decision was not a surprise. For the third time in four years, Mississippi State would turn down an invitation to the NCAA tournament because of the likelihood that it would have to face a team with black players. Kentucky, which lost two more games and won one fewer than Mississippi State, would represent the SEC in the national tournament. That's the same Kentucky that Mississippi State beat by five in Lexington less than a month earlier. Its opening game was set for March 16, 1962, against either Butler or Bowling Green State at the Iowa Fieldhouse.

Jack Berkshire and Joe Dan Gold piled into Gold's two-door 1960 Ford and drove fourteen hours from Starkville to Iowa City. They bought two tickets and wound up near the top of the gym. Below them, way below them, was the Ohio State basketball team and its stars, John Havlicek and Jerry Lucas. Their opponent was Kentucky, representing the Southeastern Conference. The champions of the Southeastern Conference—well, at least two of the five starters—were sitting up in the rafters, trying not to think about what might have been and trying to enjoy a game that they knew they should be playing, not watching.

Ohio State won by ten. "I don't know that we could have beaten them," Berkshire said, "but you never know."

Chapter 5

A HISTORIC DECISION

On the night of Sunday, September 30, 1962, U.S. marshals surrounded the Lyceum building—the historic, white-column, red brick structure at the center of the University of Mississippi's campus. Their mission was to protect James Meredith, a twenty-nine-year-old black man from Attala County who intended to enroll at Ole Miss. The court battle that led to Meredith's enrollment had occupied Mississippi's attention for months. At stake was the bastion of Mississippi society, its flagship university. The battle—a literal battle—that ensued in the quaint town of Oxford that night and into the next morning cost two lives and drew the nation's attention to Mississippi's struggles like it hadn't since Emmett Till, if ever.

In Starkville, the goings-on up the road drew plenty of attention. Mississippi State was, of course, not yet integrated. But if Ole Miss fell, Mississippi State was inevitable. Also, the students at Ole Miss were largely like the students at Mississippi State—Mississippians, many of whom were fiercely protective of their way of life. Naturally, some wanted to go to Oxford. A student leader approached Colvard to see if he would cancel Monday classes so that students could go to Oxford in support of Barnett. He declined and encouraged the student to lead by keeping the students there rather than marching off to Lafayette County. A local radio station switched its format from requests to a loop of "Dixie" for some time. Before President John F. Kennedy spoke to the nation about the crisis that night, more than one hundred Mississippi State students had gathered around the statue of Stephen D. Lee on the Drill Field, chanted and marched peacefully downtown as Colvard listened from the president's home nearby. Though Colvard wasn't completely successful in preventing activism from his own students—he claimed that thirty went to Oxford, half of them arrested—the night evaporated with no incident.[17]

The weekly student newspaper, the *Reflector*, ran an editorial on the front page of its next edition (October 4) decrying "the destruction of STATES RIGHTS." The paper wrote of "heart-stirring strains of 'Dixie' interspersed with blood-curdling Rebel yells" as students waited for the latest news out of Oxford. Inside, the editorial writer pounced on the issue in terms of his all-caps reference on the front page: "Mississippi is an individual and sovereign state; she will not allow herself to be poured into the common mold and be made powerless against the whims of the central powers. Mississippians are individuals in their own rights, and as individuals they must be allowed the privilege of solving their own problems in their own ways."

On Friday, October 6, nearly a week after the Meredith incident, a weary Colvard turned to his diary. "My heart is heavy," he wrote. "I am torn between a sense of responsibility to keep quiet and try to maintain a reasonable stability at Mississippi State University and a feeling that I should resign."[18] A month later, as Colvard spoke to the Rotary Club and the executive council of the MSU alumni association, the issue remained hot. "At this point, let me make it clear that the agitators for forced integration will receive no comfort from me. Let me also make it equally clear that I shall do everything in my power to prevent any violence from occurring on this campus resulting either from this problem or from any other. We shall need your help in keeping outside agitators off our campus."

Colvard, the North Carolinian, would find counsel and comfort in a native Mississippian, Robert H. Walkup, the minister at First Presbyterian Church. Born in 1915 in Jackson and baptized in that city's Central Presbyterian Church, Walkup grew up in Senatobia. He was an orphan by age seven, left to be raised by his maternal grandparents. His grandmother, who was actually his stepgrandmother, was a stern woman. Yet her introduction of her grandson to the classics in her library fostered an enlightenment that was the foundation of his life.

In the turbulent years, Walkup did not hesitate to massage his sometimes sharp rebuke of the state of affairs in Mississippi with a reminder that he was no outsider. He, too, was a Mississippian. As a child in Senatobia, probably not unlike many children of the 1920s and 1930s in Mississippi, he witnessed an event that would have a profound effect on his view of the race question. While returning to school after lunch, he noticed a commotion at a store.

He pressed through the crowd to see a black man dead on the floor, shot by a white man whom Walkup knew. But the man was not prosecuted for the crime, and Walkup's most stark revelation was that his grandfather, a man he respected, didn't express outrage at the shooting.

Walkup spent a year studying law at Ole Miss before following the call to the ministry. He enrolled at the Presbyterian seminary in Louisville, Kentucky, and was ordained in 1941. His first charge was a small church in Ozark, Alabama. In 1953, he became pastor at First Presbyterian in Starkville. He was highly personable, loved to tell jokes and, perhaps most importantly, kept his sermons to a tidy fifteen minutes or less.[19]

The Meredith situation, despite its blood and unease, revealed an important point to Colvard, one that would play as significant a role in his next few months as any. If the "unwritten law" existed in large part to keep Mississippi universities segregated, what was the point now that Meredith had effectively integrated them?

On October 15, two weeks after the riot at Ole Miss, Mississippi State's two-time defending Southeastern Conference basketball team started its practices in its quest for a third consecutive title, its fourth in the past five years. Babe McCarthy was not yet forty years old. Yet what he had accomplished thus far was marvelous. Two of his teams had gone 24-1. Three of his last four teams ended the year ranked among the nation's best. Adolph Rupp and Kentucky were far from an afterthought in SEC circles, but McCarthy and Mississippi State were the clear darlings. One thing was missing from that resume, and that was a trip to the national tournament.

Within the team, the year began with a sense that this would be different. It would be easy to gauge that simply from the last-chance aspect of the roster. The fantastic freshmen of the fall of 1959, the class that was recruited on the coattails of McCarthy's Bailey Howell–led team, were seniors. They had given plenty but had yet to be rewarded with the payoff. Politically, Meredith's enrollment at Ole Miss had poked a hole in the "unwritten law." Socially, opinion was turning. With each passing year of unfulfilled dreams for Mississippi State, more and more Mississippians spoke up in the team's support.

Mississippi State would have to win the Southeastern Conference, of course, for this to matter. Joe Dan Gold, Leland Mitchell, Red Stroud and Bobby Shows returned from the 1962 team, but an important member did not: Jack Berkshire, who a year earlier had exhausted his eligibility. Doug Hutton, from a town just west of Jackson named Clinton, stepped in from

Doug Hutton of Clinton wasn't offered a scholarship at Mississippi State until an amazing performance in the state high school tournament. *Courtesy of Mississippi State University Athletics.*

the role of an oft-used reserve to take over the all-important point guard job.

Hutton's road to Starkville was always what he had envisioned, beginning with one rainy Saturday afternoon in the early 1950s when he heard radio announcer Jack Cristil describe the considerable exploits of football legend Jackie Parker in a Mississippi State win. Yet his body wouldn't make the path so easy. He topped out at five-foot-eleven, which didn't make him particularly marketable to major college basketball teams. Vanderbilt offered him a scholarship, but most of his interest came from smaller schools. But playing for Clinton High School in the 1960 Mississippi state tournament at City Auditorium in Jackson, Hutton scored 47 points in a semifinal win in the morning and 54 points in a title game win in the evening. His 101-point day was witnessed by McCarthy and Simmons. Less than twenty-four hours later, he signed a scholarship agreement with Mississippi State.

Hutton was Berkshire's understudy and played quite a bit as a sophomore in 1961–62, but the two players had different styles. Berkshire focused more on distributing the ball, even to the point that some wondered why he didn't shoot as often. Scoring wasn't his priority—there were other players, like Stroud, Mitchell and Gold, who did that and did it well. Game management and defense were Berkshire's strengths. Hutton, though, was more of a scorer. He was a high-energy addition to the puzzle that already included super seniors Stroud, Mitchell and Gold.

Mitchell was the brawn and toughness that established the Bulldogs in the paint. "I use the term 'toughness,' his ability and agility to out-rebound a guy five, six, eight inches taller than him," recalled teammate Jackie Wofford. "If I could, in a very professional way, use the word 'sneaky.'" Mitchell had a knack for holding players below him with an elbow parallel to the floor, the referee none the wiser. Another teammate, Larry Lee, remembered just how perfect his timing was. "I've never seen anybody quite like that," Lee said. "He wasn't a real leaper. He didn't just jump out of the top of the gym, but on defense and rebounds and getting his shot off…his timing was as good as I've ever seen from somebody." "He was kind of our enforcer," Hutton remembered. "Now, I'm telling you, he was not afraid of anything. He came from a tough background, and he was tough, now. He was a tough customer." In 1961–62, Mitchell led the team in scoring (16.7 points per game) and rebounding (8.9 per game).

Gold was the team's unquestioned leader, McCarthy's example for doing things the right way and in earnest. "He was the calm that brought the whole group together," Wofford said. "That's what a captain should do, that's what a leader should be, and that's who Joe Dan was." He was consistent, averaging thirteen points and nine rebounds during his junior year. Said Hutton, "Every team has that guy in the middle that will step out and take that charge, and Joe Dan was our guy." Said Lee, "He may have been the glue that held that team together."

But Stroud, the redhead from Forest who said that he was a shooter—not a guard or a forward—when arriving a few years earlier, made the Bulldogs go. His two-handed set shot, almost a heave from the back of his neck, was hardly inspiring until it invariably wound up in the bottom of the net. He was a beloved teammate, too, but it wasn't because of his gregarious personality. Gold, his roommate, would often find himself hanging out in others' rooms because he couldn't get Stroud to strike up a conversation. "You'd have to be around him two years to get two words out of him," Shows recalled.

With Hutton as the new piece to the puzzle, Mississippi State's 1962–63 season began like most of the others—the Bulldogs racked up win after win after win. But unlike previous seasons, Mississippi State started the year with national recognition. State was sixth in the United Press International poll. "We've got the biggest job ahead of us we've ever confronted in living up to that high national ranking," McCarthy said. "This is the first time we've opened with national recognition already conferred on us, and it came as a reward for the fine work done by our boys during the past two seasons. Now, we must really battle to try to live up to that recognition."

In the *Clarion-Ledger*, Lee Baker wondered if State was as good as last season. Noting that four starters returned, as did six of the top seven in

McCarthy's rotation, Baker lamented the loss of Berkshire, calling him "the glue that held together" the previous two seasons. The losses of Gene Chatham, David Glasgow and David Oakley from the State bench meant that McCarthy's reserves would be greener. "Behind [Mitchell, Gold, Stroud and Hutton], well, that's where the doubts must rise," Baker wrote, noting that it put more pressure on Shows. "All in all, it boils down to a matter of Mississippi State having great promise and a few problems," he wrote. On opening night, in front of five thousand, State blasted Arkansas A&M, 90–55. "We looked ragged at times," McCarthy said. In a five-day span from December 6 to December 10, State faced Louisiana Tech, Northeast Louisiana and Louisiana College, and the smallest margin of victory for the Bulldogs against their neighboring-state foes was 19.

The 4-0 Bulldogs received their first real test on December 15, when they traveled to Jackson to take on Memphis State in the first college basketball game played at the brand-new Mississippi Coliseum at the Fairgrounds. Tickets ranged from $1.10 to $2.75. A solution that had been added to the floor to make it shine also made it slick. The can from which the solution came noted that it would dry in twenty-four hours. "It's been longer than that," the coliseum manager said. McCarthy was diplomatic. "This is a fine place," he said. "It's built exactly like the other great ones, and I don't think it would take second to any of them." In front of a crowd of 6,500, said to be the largest crowd to see a basketball game in the history of the state, State placed four players in double figures and won easily, 77–66. McCarthy noted that it was the best he had seen Gold play. Among the 6,500 in attendance was Governor Ross Barnett, who threw out a ceremonial "first ball," a heave across the floor to Mississippi State sports information director Bob Hartley.

State improved to 5-0 but would remain undefeated for only two more days. The Bulldogs flew to Blacksburg, Virginia, soon after the Memphis State win and enjoyed a promising start, leading by 9 with six minutes left in the first half. State began to lose poise and take ill-advised shots, and Virginia Tech eventually won going away, 82–65. Yet something else, something beyond just a simple lack of poise, contributed to the result. Mississippi State, with essentially every one of its players coming from Mississippi, wasn't used to being in the Appalachian Mountains. "That's about 3,800 feet, and you could tell it," Hutton recalled. "It was thin air up there."

The Bulldogs bounced back two nights later with a 106–71 demolition of Christian Brothers, broke for Christmas and then took a 6-1 record and a no. 10 national ranking to New Orleans for the Sugar Bowl tournament. Their first test was Houston, and the Cougars weren't lightweights. They pounced on State from the jump, leading 37–18 after fourteen minutes. State clawed away, though, drawing to within 1 with 1:41 left and then taking the lead, 73–71, on Mitchell's steal and three-point play with 37 seconds remaining. Yet Houston had an answer in Lyle Harper's layup with 28 seconds to play. In overtime, Harper's two free throws with 5 seconds to play clinched a 79–76 win. Mitchell, Gold, Brinker and Shows watched the end of the game from the bench; they had fouled out. The next day, State knocked off Xavier 75–66 to go 1-1 in New Orleans. On New Year's Day, the Bulldogs finished their last game before conference play by whipping Delta State, 106–77. By then, though, State was 7-2 and had fallen out of the national poll.

The other squad in the four-team Sugar Bowl tournament that year was Auburn—the team with the shuffle offense that gave the Bulldogs fits four years earlier. But ever since that first game of the 1959 SEC season, McCarthy had made strides in figuring out how to play against the shuffle. In 1961, State won by eight in Auburn, dealing the Tigers their first loss of the season. In 1962, State won by three. Yet the 1963 Tigers entered their SEC opener against Mississippi State looking a bit tougher than they did in the previous two years, even though they went a combined 33-13 in those two seasons. Auburn was 8-0 after beating Xavier (by seven) and Houston (by two, in overtime) at the Sugar Bowl tournament. The Tigers also had beaten Texas Tech and twice defeated Florida State. In this meeting, Mississippi State would be a clear underdog, which is probably how McCarthy wanted it.

Whatever the motivation, Mississippi State played that Saturday in Auburn as if it were the SEC's elite, not the Tigers. Helping the cause, Auburn shot a mere 35.4 percent from the field. Leland Mitchell scored 15 points, grabbed thirteen rebounds and missed just one of his ten free throw attempts. McCarthy said it was his greatest game. Red Stroud was seven for eleven from the field, too. Mississippi State won, 62–53. The *Clarion-Ledger's* Baker said it was "coldly precise." And because the other perceived league contenders, Georgia Tech and Kentucky, had to come to Starkville for their annual meetings with State, Baker declared that "perhaps the Southeastern Conference championship was settled here Saturday night."

If so, State didn't get the message. Neither did Alabama. Two nights later, in front of a sellout crowd at Foster Auditorium in Tuscaloosa, State started the game missing about everything it attempted. Alabama led by ten at halftime and by eight with 5:30 to play. But much like the Houston game less than two weeks earlier, State clawed back to force overtime—this time, on Hutton's jumper with a minute to go and a crucial steal by Gold with seconds remaining. In the extra period, Alabama's Reese Carr nailed two free throws with just under three minutes to play, and the Tide didn't cede the lead. "They just wanted to win more than we did," McCarthy said. "That's why they won."

Mississippi State rode its bus back the seventy or so miles down U.S. Highway 82 to Starkville that night with a respectable season under its belt. The Bulldogs had won nine times, lost three times. They had split their first two SEC games. Half a decade ago, this would have been quite the start for the Bulldogs, who at that point had never accomplished anything of note on the hardwood. But McCarthy had raised the team's expectations. And specifically for the 1962–63 team, the year before had raised the expectations to an almost illogical level. How does a team follow up a 24-1 record? By the measures of those expectations, the season was far from a success. A lofty national ranking had disappeared. The Sugar Bowl, a place where State had once been a darling, produced a measly third-place finish. And now, a loss to Alabama. If the Bulldogs could lose to the Crimson Tide, then what of the two teams heading to Starkville the next weekend, Vanderbilt and Georgia Tech? Making matters trickier was Tech's surge. The same night Mississippi State scored its big win in Auburn, Tech surprised the league with a double-overtime, 86–85 win at Kentucky. The Yellow Jackets took a 10-0 record and a no. 7 ranking in the national polls to their Mississippi swing.

For Mississippi State, though, the first task was bouncing back from that Alabama loss against a tough Vanderbilt team. The Commodores proved their worth, taking a 55–53 lead on a Roger Schurig shot with thirty-one seconds to play. McCarthy called timeout. "Boys," he said, "we've been further down than this with less time to play and still won—so don't give up." Red Stroud knocked down a jumper on the next possession to tie the game, and Vandy missed a shot on its next possession. Mitchell was fouled when he pulled down the rebound and hit the go-ahead free throws. He scored 8 of Mississippi State's final 12 points, and the Bulldogs escaped with a 58–55 win.

Tech improved to 11-0 that night by beating Ole Miss in Oxford, but it wasn't a particularly convincing win (two points, in overtime). On Monday night in Starkville, Tech and State tussled early before the Bulldogs took a 6-point lead at halftime. Behind a massive rebounding advantage, Red Stroud's hot shooting and a roaring crowd, State stretched its lead to 53–36 some six minutes into the second half. Tech pulled to within 13 with seven minutes to play before McCarthy put on the stall and watched the time run out of an 81–69 victory. Stroud scored 30 points, going eleven for nineteen from the field and making all eight of his free throws. Mitchell scored 25 and had twelve rebounds. "I knew if they got the lead and that student body got behind them, we'd have a tough time," said Whack Hyder, the Tech coach.

Georgia Tech coach Whack Hyder. *Courtesy of Georgia Tech Athletics.*

Earlier in the day, State's campus received a bit of a scare—the kitchen in the old gothic cafeteria caught fire. It didn't affect the game, but did leave a considerable amount of literary inspiration to the writers who covered it. Robert Fulton, writing in the *Clarion-Ledger*, said that "the late afternoon blaze which gutted the campus cafeteria carried over into Maroon gym here Monday night as Miss. State's revved-up Maroons gutted Ga Tech's previously undefeated Yellow Jackets 81–69 to the almost incessant thundering of 5,100 participants." The *Atlanta Constitution* noted, "In its eighth road game, Tech simply ran out of gas and was beaten by a State team as fired up as its campus cafeteria, which was destroyed by flames a few hours earlier." The *Constitution* also reported that Hyder will "be glad to see young Mr. Stroud in the graduation line this June."

Alabama's loss at Florida shored up the SEC race two weeks into it. All of the contenders had one loss, and now State had the kind of schedule that would allow it to make some hay before the annual all-important meeting with Kentucky in three weeks. Ole Miss was first up, and though the Rebels had started strong under first-year coach Eddie Crawford, they were no match for State. McCarthy cleared his bench, notched a fourteen-point win in front of a crowd of 5,100 and left Crawford scratching his head. "That Stroud is a hell of a player," Crawford said. "We knew what he was going to do and had a hand in his face almost every time he shot and still couldn't stop him."

State returned to the top 10 a week later, at no. 7 in the UPI list and no. 9 in the AP. It would be short-lived, though, as State squandered an 18-point lead and fell 71–65 to Memphis State in front of nearly five thousand at Ellis Auditorium in Memphis. State rebounded with a 62–52 win over Southern Mississippi at Mississippi Coliseum in Jackson, a game that ended when an angry Southern fan threw a chair on the floor. "The most fortunate thing that happened all night was when that guy missed me with that chair," Mitchell said. State returned to SEC play in the first week of February, dispatching LSU, 73–66, in Starkville, with Stroud making all fourteen of his free throws. Two nights later, State pulled away from Tulane and won, 91–73, behind 29 points by Mitchell. The win boosted State to 6-1 in the SEC, tied with Georgia Tech but owning the tiebreaker by virtue of the Bulldogs' early January win over the Yellow Jackets in Starkville. With Tennessee and Kentucky looming for their every-other-year weekend in Starkville, talk again centered on the NCAA tournament.

In 1959, when Mississippi State was held at home after winning the SEC for the first time, Babe McCarthy didn't make much noise. The contract extension and raise he received around that time certainly helped. But McCarthy grew increasingly perturbed in 1961 and 1962, and by 1963 he didn't mind speaking out. "Everywhere I go, people ask me the same thing," he said in late January. "In the past, I've always answered 'no comment,' but now I'm telling everybody that things look better than they ever have." McCarthy believed that 75 percent of Mississippians wanted State to go, and he said that his team ought to go if it could win its conference. "Now, since the James Meredith case at Ole Miss, they can't say, 'I told you so, you played against integrated teams and look what it brought on' because it didn't bring it on," McCarthy said.

There may have been another reason for McCarthy's brash talk. Many of those who played on that 1963 team believe that Colvard had already assured McCarthy that if his team won the SEC that year, he would see to it that it would go to the NCAA tournament. But it's hard to pinpoint when, where and how definitive such assurance was. Hutton said that he recalled Colvard coming to practice one afternoon two games into the season to tell the players that if they qualify, he would "do everything [he] can do to see that you get to go." Larry Lee, a backup on the 1963 team, remembered something similar, though maybe just in private to McCarthy. Jimmy Wise, the team's manager, recalled McCarthy telling the team that they would get to go. "Now, I might not have a job when it's over," Wise recalled McCarthy saying, "but we're going." Said Wise, "I don't know if he knew something, or if he knew the president would support him, but he had determined that he was going to do everything possible to get us in the tournament." In his diary, Colvard didn't allude to such a definitive assurance.

None of this would matter, of course, if State couldn't actually win the SEC. As they had in State's previous three SEC-winning seasons, the weekend of games against Tennessee and Kentucky would prove to be a pivot. In 1959, wins in these two games all but clinched the league title. In 1961, a loss to Kentucky was absorbed by State's big lead, but in 1962, wins at Tennessee and Kentucky again put State safely in front of the SEC pack. By the start of 1963's critical weekend, the league crown was a two-horse race between the Bulldogs and Georgia Tech, each of which had one loss. Kentucky was two games back with three losses, but it was Kentucky, after all. Tennessee and Alabama also had just three losses. State appeared destined for its second loss when the Vols led for much of the second half in front of a rabid five thousand spectators on the night of February 9, 1963, but a four-point play—a one-hand jumper by Stan Brinker and a foul on the Vols that led to two Aubrey Nichols free throws—put the Bulldogs up for good. State improved to 7-1 with a 63–59 win.

Next up, Kentucky. Though McCarthy had always preached to his team to get an early lead, it was the Wildcats who did that on the night of February 11, quickly up 4–0. But State recovered, taking a 9–8 lead that it would stretch into a 6-point halftime lead, 38–32. Gold's fifteen-footer at the halftime buzzer put the crowd into a frenzy. State held a small margin of a lead through the rest of the second half and scored the game's final field goal, a Hutton layup, with 2:55 to play. From then on, McCarthy's stall won out. State nailed its free throws—Mitchell converted two key one-and-ones—and won, 56–52. McCarthy raved about Gold's defense on Cotton Nash, who scored a mere 8 points, and praised Mitchell's passing ability. More than about anything, though, he delighted in something more personal. "I said before the game that if I could win this one I'd be even with Adolph for the first time in my life and now I am," McCarthy said. The country boy from Baldwyn had met the Baron of the Bluegrass eight times, winning four and losing four.

Now 8-1 in the Southeastern Conference, State had a clear path to the title with Georgia Tech's overtime loss to Tulane.

Mississippi State's path to the NCAA tournament was less than clear, though. Assuming that it was able to protect its essential two-game lead with five games to play, a tangle of politics, egos and the tortured policy of racial segregation made a tournament berth still a decisive underdog, no matter how headstrong Dean Colvard was or just how much Babe McCarthy was willing to risk his neck. McCarthy, though, made a savvy appeal when he spoke out about the tournament in late January: He mentioned that public sentiment appeared to be on the side of those in favor of Mississippi State playing in the tournament. Broadly speaking, he appeared to be correct. A survey conducted by WJTV and WSLI, a pair of Jackson television stations, reported that 85 percent of respondents were in favor of the team playing in the tournament. The manager of the stations sent Colvard a telegram telling him about the results.[20]

In the February 7 issue of the *Reflector*, a letter to the editor signed by seventeen alumni who were law students at Ole Miss urged those in charge to send the team. "In the opinion of these writers, which we hope is the overwhelming opinion of Mississippi State Alumni, the refusal to allow the Southeastern Conference Champions of Mississippi State University in 1959, 1961 and 1962 to participate in the NCAA tournament was nothing short of a tragedy," the letter read. It warned of tougher paths on the recruiting trail for McCarthy and pointed to other teams, such as Alabama playing an integrated Oklahoma team in the Orange Bowl, as precedent. A petition urging participation in the tournament was circulating MSU's campus and was brought to the attention of Fulton of the *C-L*. "We are for segregation," wrote the man who brought the petition to Fulton's attention, "but can see no harm in State's participating in the NCAA tournament."

Letters and telegrams poured into Colvard's office from across the state and beyond, too. On February 28, a letter signed by forty-one people urged participation. On the same day, a letter from Owen Cooper of Yazoo City supported the trip. It was also signed by the comedian Jerry Clower, who sent a letter of his own with a copy of an article he had written in the *Yazoo Herald*. The Tupelo Luncheon Civitan Club voted unanimously in favor of the trip, too. But there was sentiment against the trip as well. A Natchez couple wrote to Colvard, telling him that "if we play this game with Negroes, don't you and all others concerned know that they are going to ask for a return or some other northern team ask you to play on our own ground. If we refuse, our good President Kennedy will force us to play and accept Negroes." A school principal wrote that "all of the Mississippi people whom I have discussed this with are bitterly opposed" to the trip, and a Natchez man told Colvard that he felt that "the cheap publicity of going to the NCAA is too high a price for our self-respect and integrity."[21] Colvard apparently read them all, at least enough to surmise that "the communication pledging support tended to be less emotional and somewhat more sophisticated than those in opposition."[22]

The *Reflector*, in an unsigned editorial, seemed to support the trip—but in a way far from sophisticated:

> *The idea of not competing because in that way the Mississippi stand on integration would be harmed seems to be somewhat pig-headed. That's a rather harsh emotional way of stating an opinion, so we shall reiterate a little here and see if we can't look at this problem with cool heads and controlled hearts. First of all we approach the question of Mississippi's stand on integration and how this would be affected by our all white team competing in the NCAA tournament. Certainly it would be hard for our boys to place themselves on the same court with one of the Negroid race, since all their lives our boys have been protected from such close personal contact.*

In the *Clarion-Ledger*, sports editor Carl Walters was in favor of State going to play in the tournament. But he didn't think it was likely. "When we expressed the opinion yesterday that there is no chance for a change in the policy that has kept State out of three previous NCAA events, we were simply being realistic," he wrote. "This is an election year. Politics is heavily involved in anything that is done—or not done—in connection with the Bulldogs going to the national tourney or not going. And we doubt that those who could 'unlock the door,' so to speak, have the intestinal fortitude required for a favorable verdict."

In a restaurant in Leland, a small Delta town just east of Greenville, the opposition went beyond just editorials and telegrams. At 8:30 a.m. on the morning of February 23, a man walked into a café and asked for a petition that had been circulating advocating Mississippi State's entry into the NCAA tournament. Thinking that he planned to add his signature, the owner handed it over. Then the man asked for matches. He lit the petition on fire, dropped it on the floor and walked out without saying another word.

While the story swirled on the outside, the basketball team still had work to do. And even with the two-game cushion, it made things interesting. Mitchell, Stroud and Gold combined to miss twenty of the twenty-three shots they attempted in the first half of a February 16 game at Florida, and the Bulldogs lost by 21 to a Gators team that was 4-6 in league play and had just been beaten at Auburn by 29 points. State rebounded at Georgia two nights later, though, and notched an 86–75 win. The Florida loss, though, had eliminated much of State's margin for error.

State was given a break on February 23 when Auburn, still a contender for the crown, lost by 23 to Kentucky. That opened the door for State to regain much of its cushion in its game at LSU, and it did in a hurry. The Bulldogs were up by double digits just eight minutes in and led 57–34 at halftime en route to a 99–64 win in Baton Rouge. State missed just ten of its thirty-three shots in the first half. Seemingly buoyed by the wide margin of victory, McCarthy gave in to some NCAA lobbying. "It would be a shame for a team capable of playing as well as our boys did away from home tonight, not to get a chance to play in the NCAA," he said.

In New Orleans two nights later, McCarthy finished his end of the bargain. In a game that featured some seesaws early, the Bulldogs broke away and led by as many as 17 early in the second half and beat Tulane, 78–67, to clinch their third consecutive Southeastern Conference title. Stroud scored 28 and Gold had 26. McCarthy again stumped for his team: "It makes my heart sick to think that these players, who just clinched no worse than a tie for their third straight Southeastern Conference championship, will have to put away their uniforms and not compete in the NCAA tournament." Wrote Fulton: "So now it is the hour of decision once again for the officials who have for three years kept championship Miss. State teams at home while less worthy clubs represented the league in the NCAA. If those officials show the guts and courage displayed last night by the Bulldogs their chances of going will be greatly improved."

By the morning of February 26, the day after the win at Tulane, the decision belonged to Colvard and Mississippi's politicians. S.R. Evans, who chaired the College Board's athletic committee, said a day after the Tulane win that the state's policy hadn't changed. He said that the committee's "present feeling is that the situation won't change unless there is an expression from the legislature and the state administration in favor of a change." The committee, he said, wouldn't even entertain the question until an official invitation arrived. Bernie Moore, the Southeastern Conference commissioner, had given Mississippi State athletic director Wade Walker a deadline of Monday, March 4, two days after the season finale at Ole Miss, for an answer. The drop-dead deadline, as Colvard understood it, was Tuesday, March 5.[23]

In Atlanta, Georgia Tech waited. Whack Hyder, the Yellow Jackets' coach, told reporters that he was in favor of State heading to the tournament. But he said that his team would be "ready and eager" to go, just like it did in 1960. That's when Auburn won the SEC title but couldn't play in the tournament because it was on NCAA probation. Georgia Tech represented the SEC in the Mideast Regional at Freedom Hall in Louisville, Kentucky, beating Ohio University before losing to Ohio State.

Colvard weighed his options. He knew that navigating the waters of the legislature would be tricky. On one hand, it was an election year, and legislators would likely be quick to posture. But on the other hand, Colvard knew that meddling in university affairs by legislators would be frowned upon by accreditors, and he knew that the legislators knew this, too. As Colvard saw it, there were two options. Under the first approach, he could make a recommendation to the College Board, which would essentially force it to convene. At that point, the recommendation stood a good chance of failing. Though Colvard would follow proper procedure under this avenue, he would put the backs of his board members—his bosses—against the wall, and both he and Mississippi State would likely suffer public defeat. The second option didn't follow board protocol but was more enticing: He could preempt the board, grant full permission and take the public relations risk. Ted Martin, an advisor, argued that the board should call a meeting on its own, but Colvard knew that it wouldn't.

Colvard wrestled with the options a good two days. On Wednesday night, February 27, he phoned Walkup, the pastor, and told him of his decision. The two chatted and shared a short prayer. He called Owen Cooper, the prominent alum in Yazoo City. He called J.D. Williams, the chancellor at Ole Miss. He called the editors of a handful of influential newspapers. He told his wife, and extra security was arranged at the presidential home. On Thursday, he spoke to a group of stockholders for a New Orleans bank and received applause when the person who introduced him inferred that he hoped the team would play. On Friday, the Colvards went to Meridian for the "Johnny Baker, All-American Boy" dinner, which honored Baker, a former State football star. Ross Barnett was there, and the two exchanged pleasantries.[24]

In Oxford on Saturday night, March 2, Mississippi State continued its domination of its archrival, winning 75–72. Joe Dan Gold scored 24, including a layup early in the second half that put the Bulldogs up for good. Yet the most significant development came fifteen minutes before tipoff, when Colvard publicized his decision by releasing this statement:

STATEMENT BY
D.W. COLVARD, PRESIDENT OF MISSISSIPPI STATE UNIVERSITY
RELATIVE TO PARTICIPATION IN
NATIONAL COLLEGIATE ATHLETIC ASSOCIATION
CHAMPIONSHIP COMPETITION

This statement is the result of my best effort to do my duty, as I see it, toward the students and faculty of Mississippi State University, its alumni and friends, and the people of Mississippi. Whatever short-comings it reveals are failures in capacity or judgment. They may not rightly be ascribed to failure in desire to do the right thing.

There is obscurity about the "unwritten law." Some say it is one thing; some, another. And still others aver that it does not exist. Be that as it may, it is certain that there is precedent for the President of Mississippi State University to act in the matter of participation in the NCAA basketball championship competition. Under that precedent, I am acting with the full knowledge of the President, the Executive Secretary, and the Chairman of the Athletics Committee of the Board of Trustees, State Institutions of Higher Learning, State of Mississippi.

The Athletics Committee of Mississippi State University, representing the faculty, alumni, and students, and the Athletic Director have recommended that our basketball team be allowed to compete in the NCAA play-offs. The student senate has passed unanimously a resolution in favor of playing. A petition signed by some 3,000 students, communications from interested alumni and friends of the institutions, and resolutions from alumni chapters—all convey an overwhelming persuasion in favor of participating.

In answer to this manifestation of interest and in the light of my best judgment, it is my conclusion that as responsible and responsive members of the academic community and of the Southeastern Conference we have no choice other than to go. Accordingly, as President of Mississippi State University I have decided that unless hindered by competent authority I shall send our basketball team to the NCAA competition.

I arrive at this decision freely and independently. I make it public with highest respect for the Board of Trustees and deepest regard for the members of the Legislature. As one who has lived in the midst of Mississippians for less than three years, I am cognizant of the hazard of this action and am fully reconciled to the possible consequences of it upon my professional career.

By Coach McCarthy and through my own personal knowledge of the players, I am firmly convinced that Mississippi State University and the State of Mississippi will have reason to be proud of their representation in this national competition, that these are splendid young gentlemen as well as splendid athletes.

My conviction is that the well-trained young people of Mississippi can compete on a favorable basis, athletically and intellectually, with the best in other parts of the country and that our champions are entitled to the opportunity to compete. I am further convinced that the spirit of fair play on the part of all concerned at the scene of the NCAA play-offs will transcend whatever prejudice or bias may obtain and transmute all participants into their essential roles as champions competing for the crown.

My feeling and my faith are that the reception of our team, in recognition of their conduct and spirit, will serve to allay the concern of those who question the wisdom of the participation. My hope for the team is an enjoyable time, good, clean competition, and victory.[25]

Colvard chose the second of the two options he had been debating. The next two weeks would prove whether he chose wisely.

Chapter 6

A DRAMATIC ENDEAVOR

Above the *Clarion-Ledger*'s gothic nameplate on the Sunday morning of March 3, 1963, ran the following headline: "O.K. STATE TO PLAY IN NCAA." It referred readers to the sports section, which told of McCarthy's remarkably subdued reaction once the decision was made public in Oxford: "It's great. I'm happy we can go. The boys deserve it. They won the championship."

McCarthy had actually learned his team's fate three days earlier, when Colvard had informed him and Athletic Director Wade Walker of his decision and how he planned to proceed. In Colvard's office, McCarthy pledged that his players would behave and cause no embarrassment to Mississippi State. "I admire your heart," McCarthy told Colvard. "I am for you and the boys," Colvard responded. "Go ahead and win." Colvard had prepped the College Board, too. Member T.J. Tubb gave his statement of endorsement. S.R. Evans, the chairman of the athletic committee, said it was good but too long. E.R. Jobe told Colvard he would call him back if there were any other changes to make. J.N. Lipscomb told him he didn't like the decision but said he would back Colvard. M.M. Roberts, learning of the decision from Jobe, called the president's house on Saturday afternoon and expressed his displeasure. Dean Colvard wasn't there, though, and his wife, Martha, had to listen to Roberts's concerns, including that her husband was ruining the state of Mississippi.

Dean Colvard had to leave town that afternoon for an already-planned trip to New York to solicit a donation from the Rockefeller Foundation, but he changed course. He didn't want to leave his wife and son at home. He cancelled his plane ticket and drove them to Memphis to stay at the Peabody Hotel, paying particular attention to highway patrolmen on the drive for fear, logical or not, that one may intercept him. Colvard couldn't pick up Jack Cristil's call of the game in the car or at the Peabody, so he called his secretary, who put the phone by the radio so he could listen. Pastor Walkup called him at the Peabody and told him that he was remembering him in his prayers. The next day, his wife and son returned to Starkville, and he went on to New York for his appointment. When he walked into his room at the Waldorf-Astoria, he turned on the radio and heard a report about what he had done back in Mississippi.[26]

Yet there wasn't much of an uproar, at least not immediately. The usual suspects, such as State Representative Russell Fox of Claiborne County, derided the decision. Fox was part of creating the "unwritten law" nearly a decade earlier. "I'm afraid the decision will be misinterpreted as a sign of weakness in our stand for segregation," Fox said. "I don't think a majority of our people approve of integrated ball games." Senator Billy Mitts of Enterprise called the decision "a low blow to the people of Mississippi." He proposed a "substantial decrease" in budgetary appropriations for state universities that encourage integration and said that the state should only put natives in the presidencies of its universities. The stance denouncing the decision was even more curious because Mitts was a former MSU cheerleader.

But on the Friday before Colvard's decision became public, the state legislature had an opportunity to take a stand. A bill introduced in the Mississippi Senate requested that the College Board enforce the unwritten law. Instead of debating it and putting it up for a vote, the Senate sent it to committee, where it would surely die.

Mississippi State would take a 21-5 record to the postseason tournament—a good one, no doubt, but nothing like the 24-1 records it finished with in 1959 and 1962. Once the calendar turned to February, the Bulldogs won 9 of their final 11 games. In the United Press International poll, State was ranked no. 7, behind Cincinnati, Duke, Arizona State, Ohio State, Loyola of Chicago and Wichita State.

Unlike today's tournament, which showcases its selection process and unveils picks as a hyped component, the NCAA championship of 1963 had a preset bracket. Teams went into slots assigned by conference affiliation and geography. Mississippi State, by virtue of its Southeastern

Loyola players Ron Miller (left) and Jack Eagan receive instruction from Coach George Ireland. *Courtesy of Loyola University Athletics.*

Conference championship, would play the winner of a play-in game between the Ohio Valley Conference champion, Tennessee Tech, and a team that received an at-large berth. That team was Loyola, a private Jesuit university based in Chicago. The Ramblers, as they were called, were making their first NCAA tournament appearance, even though the team surely didn't look like it.

Loyola had turned heads throughout the season, and it wasn't just that it plowed through its campaign with twenty-four wins and two losses. It was the manner in which the Ramblers did it that earned the most notoriety. Loyola scored 100 or more points in each of its first six games. The Ramblers won their first twenty-one games, too, and the opponents weren't all pushovers. Included in that list of victims were Indiana (106–94), Arkansas (81–62), Memphis State (94–82), Marquette (twice, 87–68 and 92–90) and Iowa (86–68). George Ireland, a Wisconsin native who was an all-American basketball player at Notre Dame in the 1930s, was the team's coach. He believed in a fast-break, up-and-down the court game that utilized a full-court pressure defense. His teams at Loyola had been marginally successful through the 1950s, but it wasn't until Jerry Harkness arrived from the Bronx in 1960 and a handful of complementary players came a year later that Ireland's team burst onto the national scene. In 1962, his team won twenty-three games and lost just four, advancing to the NIT.

Harkness, a six-foot, two-and-a-half-inch forward from the New York City borough of the Bronx, was the 1963 team's leader. By the time tournament play started, he had averaged 21.4 points per game. He was undoubtedly an all-American, and he was already a Loyola legend, owning all of the school's scoring records. At six-foot-seven, Leslie Hunter was the team's athletic center who could score—16.9 points per game. But Vic Rouse, a six-foot-six forward, was the team's leading rebounder, at 11.7 per game. Ron Miller, a six-foot-two guard who played at other positions through the year, averaged 13.1 points per game. And Jack Egan, a five-foot-ten point guard, averaged 14.2 points per game. The athletic Ramblers entered tournament play averaging 94.0 points per game. No one expected Tennessee Tech to give them much problem, so the attention back in Mississippi focused on the potential of a Mississippi State matchup with Loyola, which in itself presented another confluence of events: The Ramblers were bucking convention on the basketball floor that year, starting four black players on a five-man starting lineup. In a few days, the entire state of Mississippi would know.

Given essentially two weeks to prepare, State had quite the opportunity to scout the Ramblers, rest and recuperate from the February SEC grind and generally hone its skills before the most significant game in the history of the school. But it's unclear just how much the team practiced in those two weeks or just how much that practice was focused given all that was about to happen around them. "The boys are beginning pre-tournament practice today," McCarthy said in a March 6 story in the *Clarion-Ledger*, "and they as well as I hope they won't be deprived of the opportunity to play." Jimmy Wise, the team's manager, recalled a specific scene from a practice in those two weeks that spoke to the tall order ahead of Mississippi State facing a quick Loyola team:

> *I remember him walking into practice after we knew we were going to play* [Loyola], *and I can see him doing this—he called everybody together in a circle, and he got in the middle. And he said we know who we're going to play, and we know a little bit about them, and he knew they were basically black, had one white starter, and he took that basketball and he dropped it. And he says, "Let me just say this to you: That basketball hits the floor, more than likely a guy from Chicago, Loyola, is going to have it going the other way." He was emphasizing how quick they were, and how athletic they were, and how we had to play against them to beat them.*

Though Colvard's decree seemed to clear the path for State to give it a shot against the Ramblers, the state's complicated political situation would ensure it would be no slam-dunk.

Colvard's office became deluged with letters and telegrams, each offering a take on what he did days before. In just the four days after his decision became public, Colvard received telegrams of support from alumni chapters in Madison, Forrest, George, Yazoo and Tate Counties. The president of the chapter in four coast counties wired Colvard to tell him that "my information indicates overwhelming approval on your decision allowing [the] basketball team to go to [the] NCAA [Tournament]." By Wednesday, March 6, they had encountered quite the speed bump.

Back in Starkville, the machinations of the state's political bodies were having their effect. "We'd get high because coach said we're going," recalled Shows. "And then we'd read something in the paper that said, 'No, you're not going.' It was just an emotional thing." The most significant barrier popped up in the Wednesday paper. On the front page of the *Clarion-Ledger*, above an article by Cliff Sessions of United Press International, ran this headline: "State College Board to Discuss Tourney." The IHL Board had planned a 3:00 p.m. meeting for the upcoming Saturday, and the talk was daunting. Some members of the board wanted to codify the longstanding prohibition against playing integrated teams—write down the unwritten law, so to speak—and step in and reverse Colvard's decision. Sessions wrote that "a bare majority" backed Colvard and that the Colvard supporters may just stay home to ensure that there was no quorum for the meeting. The meeting was called by five board members who had all been appointed by Governor Ross Barnett.

While Barnett was, in many ways, the state's central figure in the Ole Miss integration six months earlier, he had stayed out of the spotlight in the Mississippi State saga. That was wholly unlike Barnett, who rose to power as a trial lawyer in central Mississippi. A native of Leake County, Barnett was the son of a Civil War veteran. To help put himself through college, he had worked a number of jobs, including that of a high school basketball coach. In 1951 and 1955, he had unsuccessfully sought the governorship. In 1959, he was elected, beginning a tenure marked with defiance to the changes brought about by the civil rights movement.[27] But given the opening of a College Board meeting, Barnett finally spoke up. In a prepared statement two days before the scheduled College Board meeting, Barnett said that he supported segregation "in every phase of activity in all of our schools." That, of course, probably surprised no one.

Also not surprising was the treatment of the story by the segregationist Jackson newspapers. In attempting to whip up furor over the topic in advance of the College Board meeting, the *Daily News* committed one of the more notable acts in that dark period of southern journalism. On Wednesday, March 6, it ran a strong editorial that again opposed State's participation in the tournament. "The glitter of another basketball trophy," the editorial read, "understandably can blind a rabid basketball fan or over-eager sports writer, but it should not be so dazzling as to prompt grown men of grave responsibility to dash off into an experimental expedition that has been found time and time again to produce sordid results." So the *Daily News* urged readers to write their College Board representatives—even going to the trouble of listing each one's name and hometown. "The first likely team to be faced by the Maroon basketball club at the Michigan tournament has a first string that is all Negro. It would be most unfortunate if friction developed during this sports contest."

That was an error, though, as Loyola only had four black starters, not five. But in apologizing for the error in the next day's edition, the *Daily News* committed its eye-opening act. It not only sarcastically apologized in an editorial by saying "or maybe a lucky white boy finally graduated to the first team," it referred readers to a photo of the starters on an inside page that ran in five columns and featured Loyola's starting five. The photo drove home the point that Mississippi's beloved Mississippi State basketball team would play on the same floor as black players, and the size of the players alone probably served to add to the intimidation. The *Daily News*, two days before the College Board meeting, suggested to readers to clip the photo and send it to members of the board.

The *Clarion-Ledger* was not without its dark moments, either. A day before the College Board meeting, it ran a front-page editorial warning of the dangers of integrated athletic fields. "We play integrated teams abroad—next we play integrated teams at home—next we recruit Negro stars to strengthen our teams—and the fast cycle of integration is completed," read the editorial.[28]

Yet one act by the state's largest paper was a bright spot, even if by accident and even if it were likely not condoned by the paper's brass. In the past, Mississippi State players didn't make many waves in terms of pushing the powers-that-be to send them to the tournament. Even Bailey Howell, whose name value would have surely meant more to the state at his time than any of the 1963 players, was diplomatic. Whether the players were instructed by McCarthy, whether they were just shy on their own or whether they simply had never been asked, rarely did a Mississippi State player speak on the tournament subject. But on the very morning of the College Board's meeting, Robert Fulton ran quotes from all twelve of the team's players in the *Clarion-Ledger*. Some excerpts follow.

Leland Mitchell: "I don't see anything morally wrong with playing against Negroes, Indians, Russians or any other race or nationality. Most of the boys have already competed against them in high school or in hometown sandlot games."

Red Stroud: "Competing in the NCAA would give us a chance to win a national championship for Mississippi State. The memory of getting that chance would be a lot better than having to live with the memory of not getting the opportunity."

Joe Dan Gold: "I think our going to the NCAA would help the school's publicity. It would make the whole state of Mississippi look less prejudiced and it would make it appear the state is trying to work out a solution to its problem of competing on the same level for national championship and prestige."

Bobby Shows: "When I was young, we use [*sic*] to choose up and play against Negroes and it didn't affect us then. In my opinion, playing against them up there won't be a form of integration because we'll be playing against them and playing to beat them. I think the majority of the people want us to go. In a democracy, the majority is supposed to rule."

Stan Brinker: "I would like to go because I came from Illinois and I've played against Negroes before. After you get out on the court, they're just ball players and part of another team you are trying to beat."

Billy Anderton: "It is the main desire of every college player to go to the NCAA. That is the big thing. If you're not playing to go to a tournament, what are you playing for? I don't believe our going would bring on integration."

Was this a calculated move, arranged by McCarthy and Mississippi State to humanize the participants just hours before the board met? Was it simply an enterprising journalist coming up with a good idea on his own? Hard to say, but it was surely hard to ignore its value as the board convened to tackle the issue.

Dean Colvard and an assistant, Ted Martin, drove to Jackson on the morning of Saturday, March 9, the day of the board's meeting and checked into the Jacksonian Motel. Colvard had been taking sleeping pills to cope with the recent pressure. The success or failure of his job, his first and potentially only presidency, rode in large part on what the board would do about his decision to send the team to the NCAA tournament. Colvard had "about made up my mind to resign" if the board voted down his team's playing in the tournament. "In fact, sometimes I found myself almost wishing I would have enough opposition to give me a good reason to resign. But then, our people would express their real concern and almost plead that I take no such drastic action," he wrote in his book. Colvard and Martin lunched in their room.[29]

Meeting in a special session in a wood-paneled room on the tenth floor of the Woolfolk State Office Building, the state College Board opened with a prayer. Outside, five women appeared to present petitions against the team playing. Four picketers, identified as students from nearby Millsaps College, were dispersed by police. Inside, a motion was made and seconded to take the rare step of opening the meeting to the press. Quickly, the group got down to business. M.M. Roberts made a motion that the team not be allowed to go the tournament. "It is a great tragedy that minority pressure groups can cause people to do things they know they shouldn't do," he said. "It looks like we are about to lose our Southern way of life, but we should not voluntarily take on a situation where we are just asking for trouble." E. Ray Izard seconded the motion, sending it on to the crucial vote, where in no small way Mississippi's "unwritten law" hung in the balance.

This was as far as it went, though. Only board member Ira L. Morgan of Oxford joined Izard and Roberts in voting to keep the team at home. The other eight members—Harry G. Carpenter of Rolling Fork, S.R. Evans of Greenwood, Charles D. Fair or Louisville, Verner S. Holmes of McComb, Tally D. Riddell of Quitman, W.O. Stone of Jackson, T.J. Tubb of West Point and J.N. Lipscomb of Macon—all voted against the resolution.[30] Colvard's decision would not be overturned.

That made Roberts's next move even more curious. His plan to keep the team at home defeated, Roberts moved for the board to request Colvard's resignation. No one seconded the motion. Riddell then moved to express confidence in Colvard and his administration. Holmes gave the second, and all but Izard and Roberts voted for it.[31] The meeting, which lasted about an hour, was adjourned.

In his room at the Jacksonian at 3:45 p.m., Colvard's phone rang with the news from the meeting. Because the press was at the meeting, and thus had questions afterward, Colvard, who had been advised to stay away from the meeting, was among the last people connected with the decision to actually know what had happened.

Bill Simpson, the *Clarion-Ledger*'s reporter, wrote a lead in the paper's Sunday edition that was understated yet historic: "Mississippi's 'unwritten law' prohibiting participation of state teams in racially-mixed athletic events was breached here Saturday afternoon."

The *Daily News* did not take the board's decision well. In its editorial that ran in the Monday edition, it called the decision "a big, bald-faced blunder, dressed up like a faceless tuxedo bound for a raw-meat banquet to celebrate the debut of 'progressive education and brotherhooding' in Mississippi...

Even if the Maroons win in Michigan [it] is no guaranteed title to the world championship's glittering cup, for they have yet to engage Tougaloo and the University of the Congo." (Tougaloo College is a historically black institution in Jackson.)

Governor Ross Barnett, meanwhile, greeted the news with polite resignation. He issued a statement in which he said he hoped the team wins the championship.

Back in Starkville, Mississippi State's preparations began in earnest. When the sun rose Sunday, March 10, the day after the board's decision, the Bulldogs had four full days before they were to leave for East Lansing, Michigan. But by virtue of the bracket, State would get a break of sorts. Loyola was merely a presumed opponent at this time, needing to dispatch Tennessee Tech, the champion of the lowly Ohio Valley Conference, in a Monday night play-in game. So McCarthy and assistant Jerry Simmons flew to Evanston, Illinois, the site of the game, to scout the Ramblers. What they saw left them in awe: Loyola breezed past Tennessee Tech 111–42. The Ramblers led 61–20 at halftime and then pulled their starters when they were up 93–30 with eight minutes to play. "The finest fast-break team I ever

The 1962–63 Loyola Ramblers. *Courtesy of Loyola University Athletics.*

had the privilege of watching," McCarthy said. "My team is not big enough to cope with the likes of Loyola."

After returning to Starkville, McCarthy told *C-L* reporter Robert Fulton that Loyola is "the best basketball team we've ever played since I've been at Mississippi State." He handicapped his team's chances at 5:1. "The entire scouting report was basically Jerry Harkness," Nichols said. Although McCarthy probably didn't mind building Loyola up in an effort to motivate his team, it's not as if he was manufacturing the words. A look at Loyola's speed and athleticism surely had to discourage the coach who built much of his teams' success around methodical, slow-down play and probably gave reason for him to wonder if his Bulldogs had gotten the worst of the opening-round draws.

Mississippi State's story had captured the state's attention, so it was only natural that the newspapers reported every detail of the team's travel plans. The Bulldogs were to depart the Starkville airfield at 8:30 a.m. on the morning of Thursday, March 14, via a Southern Airways forty-passenger Martin 404 Aristocrat. At 3:00 p.m., the Bulldogs would practice on the floor where they would play their game the following night. They would spend the night at the Kellogg Center, an on-campus hotel, and would have at their disposal a brand-new set of uniforms—one maroon, one white. About 250 tickets were reserved for State fans, but those in Mississippi who couldn't make it to Michigan had nothing to fear: Jack Cristil, the team's radio broadcaster, would be in attendance.

By Wednesday afternoon, less than twenty-four hours before that Aristocrat was to take to the skies, grim news arrived in Starkville from the state capital. Two men, state senator Billy Mitts and former senator B.W. Lawson, had filed a request for a county court to issue an injunction to prevent the team from going to East Lansing. L.B. Porter, a Chancery Court judge in the tiny Newton County town of Union, had granted the men's request. Colvard got the news at about 4:30 p.m., just after he gave a quiet message of well-wishes to the team. "I could hardly believe it," Colvard recalled.[32] Mississippi State's basketball team had overcome hurdles of years of racism, dealt with a longstanding lack of institutional fortitude, endured a sea change in the attitudes of its supporters, convinced a college president to risk his job for its cause and sweated out a meeting of the very board that could fire that president and reverse his decision, and now it had, at this late hour, a court order to overcome. Even more, it wasn't as if the Supreme Court had weighed in. It was a Chancery Court judge from a tiny Mississippi town who issued his order a few counties west in Rankin County.

Lawson and Mitts's legal reasoning was suspect, but they probably knew that. Time was most important in this issue, not the ultimate matter of who was right or wrong. If the team was delayed on its trip, it simply wouldn't make the trip, thus accomplishing their goals. In their eight-page original complaint, the two men established themselves as representatives of two parties—those with interest in Mississippi State, and those who paid taxes. The latter was most important, as it established grounds for a complaint because the school was presumed to be using public money to pay for the trip. Citing Colvard's March 2 statement in which he outlined his decision to send the team, Lawson and Mitts argued that this was now Mississippi State's policy—to use public funds "to participate in athletics foreign to this State and foreign to the public policy of this State and contrary to the laws and in violation of the policies of the State of Mississippi." It further added that "the majority of citizens of this State do not [support the NCAA trip]."

The two men even referred to recent riots involving integration at Mississippi public universities—Ole Miss, though without naming it— and said that Colvard's new "policy" was not conducive to "the securing of an education [at Mississippi State] and that said announcement has caused tensions and emotions to be aroused, which will affect the conduct of the school as well as the education of a large number of students living on said campus."

Yet the complaint had two major faults. For starters, the "unwritten law" was just that—unwritten—meaning it had never formally become part of Mississippi's established public policy. Essentially, by keeping the "unwritten law" as a handshake agreement and out of the legislature years ago, it had ensured that it would not hold up in court when it was most needed. Also, it had not been established that public funds were being used to pay for the trip.

But very little of that mattered. Once Porter signed his order issuing the injunction later that day, a Mississippi court essentially ordered that the team not make its flight the next morning. In Starkville, a student body riled up by a pep rally at Lee Hall a bit earlier greeted the news with dismay. A crowd of more than one hundred State students hanged Mitts and Lawson in effigy and had to be convinced by student body president Robert Taylor not to ignite the dummies. At the pep rally, McCarthy could hardly finish some of his thoughts before the students erupted in applause. But that would be the last McCarthy would be seen for quite some time.

In a location off campus, McCarthy gathered with the university's leadership to decide what to do next. Colvard was running the operation. He had summoned a local attorney, Buzz Walker, for some advice. Associate athletic director Rabbit Brown, athletics public relations director Bob Hartley and university PR man Bob Moulder were also there. Colvard deftly acquired some money from local banks to help foot the team's bill in an effort to get around Lawson and Mitts's objection to using taxpayer money. As Walker advised, the "unwritten law" was clearly unenforceable. Walker suggested that the team should leave that night, not the next morning as was planned, for fear of the injunction server. But Colvard figured that the deputy wouldn't force the team members to do anything, for fear of public backlash. Colvard's wife, Martha, packed her husband an overnight bag, and he and an associate left Starkville for Birmingham, where they would stay overnight.[33] By leaving the state, the men would not be subject to a Mississippi court's order. At Colvard's urging, McCarthy was headed out of state, too. His wife, Laverne, packed a bag, and Simmons, the assistant coach, came by the house to pick it up.

Most of the team gathered in one player's dorm room—either Joe Dan Gold's or Leland Mitchell's, Larry Lee recalled. "Somebody had a radio, and we were listening to the radio about what all was going on," Lee said. "One guy would drift off to sleep, the next guy would drift off to sleep; next thing you know, there were a number of people lying around in one room." At one point, Leland Mitchell suggested, probably half-serious, for the team to pile into cars and get out of state, Hutton recalled. "We were told we were going," Wofford recalled. "Pack your bags one way or the other. If we have to sneak out of Starkville, we're going to go."

While the players dozed off, the late-night drama was beginning. With Colvard and McCarthy either out of state or on a highway heading that way, a sheriff's deputy from Hinds County motored to Oktibbeha County, a solid three hours away on two-lane roads, with a copy of the injunction. The deputy had to serve the two men, or at least try to, and wasn't aware of their clever escape plans. It was close to midnight when the deputy arrived and made contact with a local sheriff's deputy, Dot Johnson. The men arrived on campus shortly before midnight and knocked on Colvard's door. Martha answered and told them he wasn't at home and couldn't be contacted, and they politely left.[34] That night, the campus police occasionally patrolled the circle on which McCarthy and his wife lived, but the deputies never arrived there. Sometime after midnight, Johnson signed a piece of paper that read: "After diligent search and inquiry in my county, the within named defendant D.W. Colvard and James McCarthy can not be found."

The team did not know that the search had been abandoned, though. So when they woke up on the Thursday morning of March 14, 1963, they set into action a plan, hatched the night before, that would become the stuff of legend—and no small amount of embellishment—in the years to come. The proceedings went like this: One van of players, the ones most likely not to play, would head to the airport first thing in the morning, driven by trainer Dutch Luchsinger. A second van, which held the more important players and Assistant Coach Jerry Simmons, stayed on campus. (A third van carried the team's luggage.) Luchsinger's duty was to arrive at the airport and ensure that the plane had arrived and that the coast was clear. If so, he would call back to Simmons and tell him to drive the four or so miles to the airstrip on Starkville's west side. But if the coast wasn't clear? Some remember there being a plan to have a *second* plane at *another* airstrip, a more spartan one on Starkville's east side—or maybe the airport in Columbus. That way, Luchsinger and his crew of second-string players could be sacrificed in order to allow the first-string players, along with Simmons, to sneak out of town. (Remember, McCarthy is waiting on the team in Nashville.)

Luchsinger struck out to the airport with Billy Anderton, Howard Hemphill, Larry Lee, Don Posey and Jackie Wofford. Upon arrival, though, there wasn't a commotion. It's unclear if the sheriff's deputy was there waiting to serve his papers. The *Clarion-Ledger*, which likened the story to an escape from Alcatraz, had perhaps the most plausible explanation. Thanks to heavy fog, the plane was delayed in its arrival from Atlanta. So when the deputy arrived, he saw neither a plane nor the team and simply departed. When Luchsinger's van arrived, the coast was clear—all except for the plane. He drove back to campus and then received word that the plane was landing. Instead of returning alone, Simmons drove his van, too, since there was no sign of trouble during Luchsinger's first foray to the airport.

Though Colvard wasn't there, he noted in his diary that officials did meet the team at the airport.[35] The *Commercial Appeal*'s Charles Love, one of four reporters embedded with the team on its trip, said that Johnson was there to serve the papers. Bob Hartley, the school's sports publicist, asked Johnson to whom he was to serve the papers. Colvard and McCarthy, he was told. Hartley then told the deputy that they weren't here. Without any other names on the injunction, the deputy was then powerless. The team was free to board the plane.

At 9:44 a.m., the Mississippi State men's basketball team was in the air, heading to play in its first NCAA tournament game. "Now I know how those East Berliners feel when they make it past the wall," one player said.

After stopping in Nashville to pick up McCarthy and Athletic Director Wade Walker, the plane headed north toward East Lansing. At the airport there, an enthusiastic delegation waited to see if and when the Mississippians would arrive. The news of the court injunction had made its way north, of course, and the tournament's organizers were tense. Mississippi State, after all, had already been printed in the tournament program. At three o'clock, the team landed, and an employee of the airport was first to board the plane. "There are all kinds of people looking for you out there," the employee told McCarthy. "Yeah," he responded. "There were all kinds of people looking for us back where we came from, too." Jimmy Wise, the team manager, was the first person to walk down the plane's stairs. A band was waiting near the plane, and one of the band's members walked over to him. He asked Wise where he was from. Wise responded that he was, indeed, from Mississippi State. The band member walked back to his group, said a few words, and began to play the State fight song, "Hail State." The band had also learned the music to "Rambling Wreck from Georgia Tech," too, just in case.

In front of a crowd of 12,143 at Michigan State University's twenty-three-year-old Jenison Fieldhouse, the much-anticipated Mississippi State–Loyola game began with a handshake. Joe Dan Gold, the white Mississippi State forward from Benton, Kentucky, reached across the center circle and shook hands with Jerry Harkness, the black Loyola forward from the Bronx. It was a moment captured for the ages. In tune with the news of the moment, the camera men with their gigantic flashbulbs all jockeyed for the image. "The gym just lit up from all these flashbulbs," Lee recalled. It was at that moment, Gold recalled years later, that the gravity of the event hit home.

The picture became perhaps the most lasting image of not just the game but Mississippi State's golden era of basketball. Look closely into the crowd, though, and there's another homage to the start of the era. Bailey Howell, the all-American from the late 1950s, the star player on a 1959 team that went 24-1 and had no chance to experience a moment like this, was sitting a few rows up. He was playing professionally for the Detroit Pistons at the time, living just ninety or so miles away, and had the night off. McCarthy snagged tickets for him, his wife and fellow Piston Jack Moreland and his wife. McCarthy also thought of Kermit Davis, Howell's teammate on that 1959 team and his first recruit at Mississippi State, offering him a seat on the team plane. Davis couldn't go, though. He was coaching at Tupelo High, and the tennis team required his presence. He, like presumably a significant portion of Mississippi, listened to Jack Cristil's call of the game on the radio.

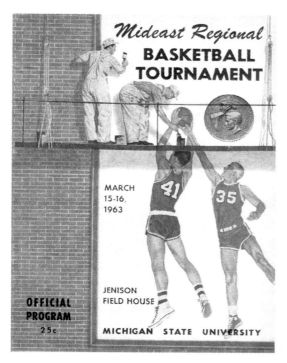

Cover of the game program from the 1963 Mideast Regional at Michigan State University's Jenison Field House. *Courtesy of Mississippi State University Athletics.*

Historic handshake aside, the game started off as well as possible for the Bulldogs. Doug Hutton laced a jump shot twenty-five seconds in, then two Mitchell layups and a Stroud free throw gave State a 7–0 lead a little under six minutes in. McCarthy, true to form, implemented his trademark stall offense.

But against a Loyola team that was long, athletic and, most of all, fast, it wouldn't work. It backfired. The Ramblers eased back into the game and, thanks to two straight 3-point plays by Jerry Harkness, tied it at 12–12 at the midway point of the first half. "There's no doubt that they were just more athletic than we were, basically," Hutton recalled. McCarthy abandoned the stall in favor of a shuffle offense. Still, Loyola kept coming. The Ramblers took the lead on a jumper by John Egan with 7:01 left in the first half and then extended their lead to 26–19 at halftime as State became faulty at the free-throw line. The Bulldogs missed six free throws in the final 10 minutes of the half.

The second half started even more miserably for State, which soon found itself down double digits. Red Stroud, the always dependable sharpshooter for the team, was having trouble finding his shooting stroke, but one jumper, coupled with a Hutton one, pulled State out of its funk and closed to within 30–27. Loyola, a team dangerous because of its quick-scoring bursts, found another one and expanded the lead to 41–31. State, again, made a run. Leland Mitchell was having a hot scoring night, and his two jump shots and Stan Brinker's 3-point play narrowed the Loyola lead again to 3, at 41–38, with 10:55 to play.

Yet disaster soon arrived. Mitchell, the team's most consistent contributor that night with 14 points and eleven rebounds, fouled out. Without him,

A Loyola player drives past three Mississippi State players. *Courtesy of Mississippi State University Athletics.*

the Bulldogs were worn down by Loyola's persistent up-and-down game. By the three-minute mark, the game was essentially over. Loyola led 57–42, and went on to win, 61–51. Mississippi State's much-celebrated trip to the NCAA tournament ended with just one game in the championship bracket. Loyola was just too much.

"We needed a perfect game to win," McCarthy said, "and didn't get it."

The box score told the story. Red Stroud finished three for fifteen shooting. "Not practicing kind of left Red rusty," Mitchell said. "That night, the ball was going in the goal and reverberating back and forth and coming back out." Mitchell fouled out. State went just six deep. Shows didn't play. "And I have no earthly idea why," Shows said decades later. "Coach never told me, never said anything." State missed nine of its twenty free throws. Harkness, as expected, led Loyola with 20 points off seven of eleven shooting. Vic Rouse had a whopping nineteen rebounds, which exposed another key element: Loyola was just too good on the glass. The Ramblers outrebounded Mississippi State forty-four to twenty-five.[36]

Mississippi State's Leland Mitchell driving to his right toward the basket in the NCAA tournament loss to Loyola. *Courtesy of Mississippi State University Athletics.*

Yet the basketball game was just that—a basketball game. It was nothing more, which allayed fears, spoken or not, among some that there could be some less-than-sporting activity on the floor when the team from Mississippi played the team from Chicago with four black players in the starting lineup. "One of the things that came out of this game was the fact that you didn't see any pushing, shoving or needling among the players," said George Ireland, the Loyola coach. "That shows that Mississippi State has a good bunch of kids, just like we have." Said Hutton, years later, "I remember how nervous and wondering how things are going to happen out as we start the game. But once you got into the game, you know, you didn't notice the color of the skin. You noticed how they could jump, you know."

Mississippi State did not immediately board the team plane and return to Starkville. In those days, a consolation game was played. For the Bulldogs, this meant a meeting with Bowling Green State, which had beaten Notre Dame in a play-in game but lost by 3 to Illinois in the same round as Mississippi State's loss. Bowling Green came from the small Ohio town of

Left: Mississippi State's Leland Mitchell finds the basket in State's consolation-round win over Bowling Green State. *Courtesy of Mississippi State University Athletics.*

Below: The 1962–63 Southeastern Conference champion Mississippi State team. *Courtesy of Mississippi State University Athletics.*

the same name, but it did have one claim to fame: forward Nate Thurmond, who was one of the best players in the country. It mattered little, though, as Mississippi State salvaged its trip up north with a 65–60 win—despite not scoring a field goal in the final twelve minutes. Thurmond had 19 points and a whopping thirty-one rebounds for a Bowling Green State team that attempted eighty shots and made just twenty-one. State, which played without Joe Dan Gold, who had broken his hand the night before, got 23 points from Mitchell.

Mississippi State's season ended with twenty-two wins, six losses and enough drama over the course of just two weeks to fill an entire season. Mitchell and Stroud were first-team all–Southeastern Conference selections by both the AP and the coaches' votes; Gold was a third-teamer. Converse named Stroud to its all-American second team; it said Gold was an honorable mention. McCarthy won his third consecutive SEC Coach of the Year award. On Sunday, March 17, just three days after a cloak-and-dagger exit from the Starkville airport, the team arrived back home. About one thousand fans were there. Players signed autographs and dignitaries spoke. Some seventy telegrams greeted the team as it departed the plane, from such far-flung entities as Tubb, the College Board chairman; Rupp, the Kentucky coach and McCarthy rival; and the entire LSU student body.

Reactions continued to pour into Colvard's office. Most of them were positive. "I do hope this action means that when the time comes for State to accept a Negro as a student our college will be spared a repeat of the unfortunate spectacle which transpired at our sister institution," wrote a man in Baltimore. "It is my guess that within five years, several of the Southeastern schools will be playing Negroes on the football teams," wrote a man in Meridian. On stationery from the Hotel Miramar in Malaga, Spain, came this note from a West Point woman: "While vacationing in Spain my brother and I were both delighted to hear your courageous decision had been upheld by the State College Board." Two letters arrived to Colvard as copies of letters sent to Mitts, the state senator who proposed blocking the team from participating. "I respect your right as a citizen to disagree," one read. "At the same time I detest your arrogant attitude and your self-centered thinking." Colvard received mail from African Americans, too. The owner of a black radio station in Newark, New Jersey, sent a letter of support and a copy of the script that had been read on its station in support. One letter appeared to just be from an earnest citizen: "I am a Negro teacher in the city of Washington, D.C. Your announcement that your university had decided to toss aside the state's 'unwritten law' banning athletic competition with Negroes is a heart-warming thing. I feel that you have done a magnificent thing."[37]

From Jackson on March 4, two days after Colvard's decision was made public, came this support:

I simply want to express to you my approval of your decision with respect to the participation by the Mississippi State University basketball team in the NCAA play-off. This is the kind of forthright and realistic approach that more of us need to adopt in our state. I can assure you of my backing and support in this and all other decisions to enable our institutions to compete effectively in both the athletic and academic spheres. Please call on me if I can ever be of any service to you in any way. With best wishes, I am Your friend, William Winter.[38]

Winter was the state tax collector. (In 1979, Winter was elected governor.)

The president of Michigan State offered his support, as did the president of the University of Wyoming. The north wing of the third floor of Smith Hall offered twenty-nine signatures in different-colored ink. An alderman in Philadelphia expressed support, as did the news director of a Jackson radio and TV station, the chairman of the Ole Miss liberal arts college, a state representative from Maben and a 1931 Ole Miss graduate living in Kosciusko.

The nastiest ones came mimeographed, with the familiar faded blue typewritten letters. A flier called "Citizens of Mississippi," signed by "Sons of Mississippi Rebel Underground," noted "Comrade Colvard and his puppet McCarthy have done an astounding job of misleading a large number of students at MSU...Any citizen of Mississippi who knowing[ly] supports an act to integrate our school as playing basketball as niggers cannot help but live in shame. A severe blow has been made at our great way of life in Mississippi." Another mimeographed flier arrived in all caps: "61–51 NIGGERS-NIGGER LOVERS MSU, BEING THE FIRST MISSISSIPPI SCHOOL TO BE DEFEATED BY A BUNCH OF NIGGERS, HAS CAUSED OUR FOREFATHERS TO TURN OVER IN THEIR GRAVES." Mailed from Jackson on March 17, two days after State's loss, with no return address, was a clipping of an account of the game with this: "State deserved this. We're happy NAACP WON."

The day of Colvard's decision, an envelope arrived from Jackson with no return address. In it, there was a photo of five scantily clad black people with guns running through a jungle, with the headline, "JOIN THE NAACP TODAY!" A card attached told Colvard that one dollar had been contributed in his name to the NAACP. "Congratulations...You Are Now An 'HONORARY NIGGER.'" In early April, an order form for courses on African languages arrived from Yazoo City, with no return address. Letters critical of Colvard's decision came from Carrollton ("May the Lord have mercy on your soul," one read), Greenwood, Learned, Carthage, Florence, Jackson ("Are you going to allow integrated teams to play in Starkville or Jackson? If so, where will the teams sleep and eat and so on?"), Sibley, Amory and Clarksdale.

Some of the letters against participation were barely comprehendible. On March 5, three days after Colvard's decision was made public, the chairman of the board of Mississippi Steel Corporation telegrammed to say that it was stopping its donations to the university's foundation. The chairman was urged to reconsider, and letters arrived to Colvard from shareholders who received a copy of the original telegram to tell Colvard that the chairman didn't speak for them.[39]

Though Colvard took note of his correspondence, he took leave of Starkville the weekend of the Loyola game. He had planned to attend the Mississippi Education Association's meeting in Jackson but remained out of state to avoid the court order. Family met him in Chattanooga, and the Colvards spent a day with their daughter in Western North Carolina before traveling to Auburn on the eve of that school's graduation. After dinner with friends on Saturday night, the Colvards went back to their hotel room, where they received a call from the Auburn president inviting them to come to his home. There, they discussed the situation over cocktails. "As we returned to the campus on Monday, March 18, we felt again somewhat like fugitives coming out of hiding. While I did not like the cloak-and-dagger operation, the unplanned scenario seemed to have been played out about as well as we could have expected," he wrote.[40]

On Thursday, March 14, likely in the time that the basketball team was in the air flying to Nashville and East Lansing, Robert Gillespie, an associate justice of the Supreme Court of Mississippi, suspended the injunction against Colvard and McCarthy. It was "issued without authority of law and was improvidently issued without notice," Gillespie wrote. Ten days later, after a hearing, the order was dismissed.

After dispatching Mississippi State, Loyola, the tiny private school in Chicago, defeated the University of Illinois the next night to advance to the Final Four. There, it demolished Duke, 94–75, setting up a title game match against Cincinnati. The Bearcats were brutal from the beginning: Loyola found itself in a fifteen-point hole early in the second half, and Harkness hadn't even scored a point. Yet the Ramblers kept clawing. Harkness found his game, capping off a wild comeback with a twelve-footer with four seconds remaining that sent the game into overtime. Tied at 58 in the final seconds, Les Hunter rose to take the game-winning shot. It bounced out, but Vic Rouse leapt up and tipped the ball into the basket as the buzzer sounded.

By a score of 60–58, Loyola won the national championship.

Chapter 7

IN THE YEARS THAT FOLLOWED

Mississippi State's success in 1963 would prove to be its last for a long, long time. The Bulldogs experienced a marked turnaround the very next season, limping to just 9 wins and 17 losses; they went 4-10 in conference play. In 1964–65, Coach Babe McCarthy's tenth season, they had just a one-game improvement, going 10-16. That would be the extent of how long McCarthy would coach at State.

One night in the winter of 1964–65, Laverne McCarthy got into the family car and lay in wait outside her husband's office on campus. She watched Babe get into his car. She watched another woman get into the passenger's seat. She followed them down the road leading out of town just long enough to realize what was going on. "They asked him to resign," she said. "It's not like back then; it's not like it is now where you could get away with things like that."

On March 3, 1965, four days after Mississippi State ended its season with a one-point overtime win at Ole Miss, the Jackson papers carried the news of McCarthy's resignation. "Today I feel that I can no longer do my best at this great institution. I leave with a heavy heart, but with malice for no one," McCarthy was quoted as saying in a statement. A United Press International story noted that "no reason was given for the resignation of the 41-year-old coach," but it reported that his statement "gave little doubt that the resignation was not altogether his own idea." Said McCarthy, "I came here with the understanding that I was to produce or else." Lee Baker of the *Daily News* called him "the greatest basketball coach Mississippi State ever had—and probably ever will."

Baker speculated that McCarthy would reenter private business, and he was right, at least for a while. During the winter of 1965–66, just three years after leading Mississippi State to the NCAA tournament, Babe McCarthy sold insurance.

Jerry Simmons, McCarthy's right-hand man over the past ten years, said that he wasn't interested in succeeding him. Popular speculation in the Jackson papers focused on Bob Vanatta, the head coach at Missouri. Vanatta had coached at Memphis State from 1956 to 1962, leading the Tigers to three National Invitation Tournaments, including one NIT final, and the 1962 NCAA tournament. Vanatta apparently talked to State athletic director Wade Walker but later withdrew his name. The *Clarion-Ledger* noted that he "was believed to be first choice." Though young, some of McCarthy's former players' names entered the speculation machine. Bailey Howell was a logical choice, but he was still under contract with the Baltimore Bullets and had already played in four National Basketball Assocation All-Star games. He told the Associated Press that he was "at the peak of my game." Kermit Davis had already taken Tupelo High to two state tournaments in three years, so his consideration was logical. Joe Dan Gold, a key member of the 1963 team and McCarthy's freshman coach the past two years, received McCarthy's endorsement. "I have the utmost respect for that young man," McCarthy said. "At times people can't see the forest for the trees. Sure he's young but has had two fine freshman teams."

On March 6, 1965, Mississippi State announced Gold's hiring. He was 39-9 in two years as State's freshman coach. He was twenty-three years old. Baker, in the *Daily News*, called the hiring a "gamble."

In the summer of 1965, Mississippi State admitted its first black student, Richard Holmes of Starkville. Though law enforcement was on alert, he entered the second summer term without incident.[41]

Such peaceful integration was due in no small part to Dean Colvard, whose decision to send his basketball team two years earlier became a point of pride for progressives in Mississippi. Naturally, his departure would become a point of sadness for them, too. It came early in 1966, the result of a call from his home state that Colvard could not resist. A year earlier, a municipal two-year college became the University of North Carolina–Charlotte, with plans to issue master's degrees by the end of the decade. Leaders asked Colvard to shepherd the transition, and he accepted.

Colvard continued as UNCC's president until 1978, at which point he retired and became chancellor emeritus. His 1985 memoir, *Mixed Emotions: As Racial Barriers Fell, a University President Remembers*, is a compelling view of

The Colvard Student Union in the center of Mississippi State's campus. It received a renovation in the mid-2000s.

how he handled the tense situation in 1963. Colvard died in 2007 at the age of ninety-three. An academic building at UNCC and the student union at Mississippi State are named in his memory.

"He was my hero, in terms of his leadership, his integrity, his intellectual integrity, and the standard he set as a university president," said William Winter, Mississippi's governor in the early 1980s and a confidant of Colvard's during the early 1960s.

Bob Walkup, Colvard's pastor at First Presbyterian in Starkville and another confidant in those tumultuous years, left the church in 1964. A year earlier, in the summer after the basketball team's trip to East Lansing, the congregation grappled with the issue of whether church services were open to people of all races. Initially, the church voted that they were. That didn't go over well, particularly outside the church walls. So the consideration was voted on a week later and soundly reversed. Only four members kept their original stance in favor of open services. Walkup was crushed.

His career took him to Memphis; Helena, Arkansas; and Auburn, Alabama, before he died in 1992. The Starkville church held a service in his honor. His ashes were buried in Senatobia.[42]

In a funeral home chapel in Benton, Kentucky, shortly after lunch one spring day in 2011, the only black man in the room walked slowly down the aisle to pay his respects. It did not take long for him to be recognized. Larry Templeton, the former Mississippi State athletic director who as a teenager had watched the teams play, walked up to visitor Jerry Harkness and made sure that he felt welcome. The two inched toward the casket, and Harkness, the star of the Loyola team in 1963, paid his respects to the grieving widow. Templeton ushered Harkness into a side room, and when the service started, he walked back down the aisle in company with a host of graying former Mississippi State basketball players.

At Joe Dan Gold's funeral, almost fifty years after the two men shook hands and the flashbulbs popped and another puncture was applied to Mississippi's old ways, Jerry Harkness was an honorary pallbearer. It was not a token gesture. When the NCAA gathered the two teams in Detroit in 2008 for recognition on the occasion of the game's forty-fifth anniversary, the two men reconnected. They were fast friends, speaking on the phone often. Gold even drove to Indianapolis once to visit. "How amazing was that? With all this story, the friendship and the relationship that they seemed to have," Gold's widow, Rosemary, recalled about a year after his funeral. "It was almost like everything came full circle, you know?"

Beside a picture of Gold by the casket and a white jersey with "STATE" written across the front, Bailey Howell read from Matthew 5 and II Corinthians. Wiping sweat off his brow with his handkerchief, the preacher read from I Samuel. Joe Dan Gold, he said, was occupying a new chair in heaven even as he spoke. Many of his former Mississippi State teammates, some of whom flew in a private plane from Starkville that morning, occupied the front pews on the left. Harkness sat in the middle of them.

To an involved Mississippi State fan, perhaps the most painful realization upon learning about the glory of the late 1950s and early 1960s is just how long it took for the success to return. Not until 1991—a span of twenty-eight seasons—did Mississippi State make its second appearance in the NCAA tournament.

Mississippi State's "gamble" on hiring Gold was unsuccessful. He had but one winning conference record in five years, a 10-6 mark his first season. Against Kentucky, the school his teams had epic battles with as a player, he was 1-8. In his final season, 1969–70, his team went 6-18, 3-15 in the SEC, and it committed the unforgivable (and rare) sin of losing twice to Ole Miss. He was dismissed after the final game of the season. He won 51 games and lost 74.

State next turned to another former McCarthy player, Kermit Davis. His first season was a pleasant surprise as State went 15-10 and broke even in 18 conference games. Though his teams were mostly respectable, they never were SEC contenders like they were when he and Howell and Keeton were playing. After finishing the 1976–77 season losing 11 of its last 14 games, Mississippi State and Davis parted ways. His teams won 91 games and lost 91. McCarthy's impact on the Mississippi State program was unmistakable. From 1955 to 1977, either he or one of his former players coached the team.

State replaced Davis with Ron Greene, who coached State to its best SEC season since the McCarthy era and eventually left to take the head coaching job at Murray State the next season. Not until the Richard Williams era in the 1990s would State return to prominence. The Bulldogs shared the 1991 Southeastern Conference title and earned their first NCAA tournament berth since 1963. (Their trip to Syracuse, New York, to face Eastern Michigan in the first round was undoubtedly less dramatic than the one twenty-eight years earlier.) In 1995, State broke through to be one of the final sixteen teams standing in the NCAA tournament, and a year later it advanced to the Final Four. Williams resigned two years later, but it's worth noting an early influence on his career—as a college freshman in Starkville in the fall of 1963, Williams often sat in the bleachers and watched McCarthy conduct practice.[43]

There remains a considerable "what might have been" element to Mississippi State's four SEC titles in five years. Though the 1963 team was undeniably strong, what with the senior leadership of players who had already won two SEC titles, some wonder if State's NCAA tournament fortunes could've been different if the 1959 or 1962 teams—both of which ended the season with just one loss—could've played. Few are willing to stake a claim on which team out of the four SEC title teams was the best one. But many then quickly return to wishing that Howell, one of the best players in the nation in 1959, could've had a chance to put his team on his back and make a run at a national title.

"We look back, and we wonder, what kind of impact could that have had on Mississippi State basketball?" Hutton said.

J.D. Gammel, the former player and freshman coach, has a more sobering, longer-term view: "I have no doubt that not only would there have been a national championship, I believe there would have been multiple national championships…Had we gotten the national coverage, it would have made a real difference the next ten or twenty years of the talent that you would have been able to attract to Mississippi State."

Mississippi State's four Southeastern Conference titles in five years are displayed prominently in the rafters of Humphrey Coliseum.

For his role in the 1961 point-shaving scandal, Jerry Graves was not allowed to play in the NBA. He became a teacher and coach in his hometown of Lexington, Tennessee. Then he became an elementary school principal and a high school principal and was elected for twelve years as the local superintendent of schools. He maintained that despite having contact with the shaving ring, he never shaved points. "I'm sorry I did it," he recalled in the summer of 2012, more than half a century after the point-shaving news hit the papers. "I wouldn't do it again, I didn't hurt my teammates and I did everything I could to win, and that's all you could ask."

Though he sold insurance in the winter of 1965–66, McCarthy's coaching career was far from over. In the spring of 1966, he accepted the head coaching position at George Washington University in Washington, D.C. For the sake of her two growing boys, Laverne moved with him. In 1966–67, McCarthy coached the Colonials to a dismal 6-18 record. But his reputation as a coach, pinned almost solely on his great run at

Mississippi State, wasn't tarnished. When the New Orleans Buccaneers of the upstart American Basketball Association (ABA) needed to hire their first coach in time for the 1967–68 season, McCarthy was their man. So he moved back down South, and once the kids were out of school, his family joined him.

The Buccaneers moved to Memphis in the summer of 1970, and McCarthy moved north with the team, remaining as its head coach. But Laverne and the rest of his family stayed in New Orleans. The two had separated. McCarthy coached the Memphis team through 1972 and then spent the 1972–73 season with the Dallas Chapparals. Shortly thereafter, the University of Georgia had an opening and offered McCarthy the chance to return to the Southeastern Conference. He snatched it up, moving to Athens, Georgia, in the spring of 1973. He even coaxed his former point guard, Jack Berkshire, to join him as an assistant. One day that fall, Berkshire was recruiting in Chicago and received a call from Athens. McCarthy had resigned to return to the ABA, this time for the Kentucky Colonels, before ever coaching a game for the Georgia Bulldogs. "Everybody was really upset at him at Georgia," Berkshire recalled.

In the spring of 1974, after his only season coaching the Colonels, McCarthy learned that he had colon cancer. He resigned his job, moved back to Baldwyn to live with his sister and had surgery at the hospital in Tupelo. Davis was with him just before he was wheeled into surgery. "Kermit," McCarthy said, "it's just a five-minute overtime."

McCarthy grew weaker over the weeks and months he stayed in his old town. But he had basketball. On occasion, he walked over to the high school gym, where he would sit on the front row of the bleachers while a young coach named Larry McKay conducted practice. "Now, you talk about intimidating," McKay said.

One late winter day in 1975, McCarthy walked to the Main Street corner where the dry goods store once stood. What passed for bustle in Baldwyn had long passed; this was a late Sunday afternoon. Simon Spight, his former pupil, happened to drive by and see him. So he stopped.

"Coach, what in the world are you doing up here?" he asked.

"Well, Spight, I just wanted to get one more good look at the old town," McCarthy said. Time was running out for McCarthy; tributes were hastily arranged. At Mississippi State, a towering, ten-thousand-seat arena was nearing completion. So, for the final game in the old gymnasium, it would be Babe McCarthy Day. Adolph Rupp, among others, was scheduled to attend. But McCarthy could not. He phoned that afternoon to say that he was too frail to make the trip. The McCarthy tribute went on, though. McCarthy, via audio tape, said in a hoarse voice, "I want to thank you for making this night possible. It's a great, great tribute to me. I hope those years of SEC championships will always stay there behind the basket." Rupp, who years earlier was the beneficiary of a skunk placed under his seat, was cheered this time and lined up on the floor beside the star players of McCarthy's day. Jim McCarthy stumbled through a few words thanking State on his father's behalf. The result of the game was unlike those of McCarthy's era: Kentucky won, 118–80.

Ten days later, McCarthy was inducted into the Mississippi Sports Hall of Fame. In front of a crowd of four hundred at a Jackson restaurant, Jim McCarthy had "eloquent words," Carl Walters wrote, speaking of how his father's grim diagnosis had brought the two men together. Indeed, Jim McCarthy found a new appreciation for his father in the nine months he would visit him in Baldwyn, and one might be safe to assume the reverse was true as well. Babe wasn't the most present father. While his children were growing up in Starkville, Laverne did the heavy lifting, as well as pressed his suits and shined his shoes.

"That was his life, coaching," Laverne McCarthy said. "That's all. That was the main thing in his life. He really didn't have that much to do with bringing up the kids or anything else. He was always focused on that basketball." His children realized the effects. By the time Jim entered college, the relationship with his dad wasn't the best. Sometimes, when he would go to New Orleans Buccaneers games to watch his dad coach, he would buy his own ticket, a protest of sorts. But he still went. "I still loved my dad," he said.

On March 18, 1975, early on a Tuesday morning, James Harrison McCarthy died. He was but fifty-one years old. His son's phone rang in his home in Metairie, Louisiana, at 5:00 a.m., just three hours after he had arrived back home after the Mississippi Sports Hall of Fame ceremony. Jim called Laverne, who dutifully reported to work a few hours later. Her boss told her to return home.

The funeral three days later was held in Baldwyn, four blocks from the high school gym. The sun was shining after consecutive days of rain. Bailey Howell and Kermit Davis were among the pallbearers. Winter, the soon-to-be governor, was there. So was Vanderbilt coach Roy Skinner. Babe McCarthy, the man who set Mississippi State on fire, the native son whose savvy with a sport helped break a barrier in Mississippi's most tortuous struggle, was laid to rest at the town cemetery, atop a rise on a winding street southeast of town, beneath a small, flat tombstone.

Grave of Babe McCarthy in the cemetery outside Baldwyn, Mississippi.

"I still loved Babe, and I still, to this day, I was really in love with him," Laverne McCarthy said one summer day in 2011. "That's the only guy I ever really went with. He broke my heart, but I forgave him."

McCarthy's final year was also the last one in which his Bulldogs would play at the New Gym. In 1975, following his death, it was renamed McCarthy Gym in his memory. It served as the home of intramural sports until 1999, when it was renovated and reopened as an indoor home for State's men's and women's tennis teams. A master plan for State's campus calls for the building to be demolished and eventually replaced with academic buildings around a green space to be named "McCarthy Quadrangle."

Since 1975, State has played basketball at Humphrey Coliseum, named after former university president George Duke Humphrey. In 2011, the school hung a banner at the north end of the coliseum's rafters commemorating McCarthy.

Almost to a man, every person involved in the 1963 team said that it never occurred to them in the moment that it was a big deal. It was just basketball, after all. And back then, going to the NCAA tournament wasn't as important as it is now. "Back when you're a young kid, going to college and doing what

116

In the 1950s and 1960s, this was home to Babe McCarthy's basketball teams. But after a late 1990s renovation, it's the indoor home of the school's tennis teams. Much of the building, though, appears to be largely the same from the time McCarthy's teams played there.

Banners in the north end of the rafters of Humphrey Coliseum commemorate star Bailey Howell, Coach Babe McCarthy and their radio broadcaster, Jack Cristil.

A late 1980s reunion of members of the 1962–63 Mississippi State Bulldogs. *Courtesy of Mississippi State University Athletics.*

you wanted to do, enjoying playing basketball, you don't really think about those issues," Nichols said. "In all fairness to the event…the social issues were furthest from our mind. We never talked about it, we never dealt with it, and it was just not important to us…We wanted to play the game."

Yet the gaze of history reveals its soothing importance at a time Mississippi needed it most. No, the Mississippi State basketball team, making a mark of progressiveness less than six months after that nasty scene in Oxford, did not cure racism in Mississippi. Medgar Evers was still alive when the Bulldogs played Loyola, and the three civil rights workers found beneath an earthen dam in Neshoba County in the summer of 1964 had probably yet to even hear of Philadelphia. But the Bulldogs, in some small way, showed what was possible. They chiseled a significant crack in the establishment.

Perhaps more than anything else, they related the absurdity of segregation in the most common of ways—through sports. "It probably did more to help the segregation situation and integrate it than any other one event, because people could relate to it," said Jack Cristil, the team's venerable radio voice. Just consider how overwhelming public sentiment for their entry into the

118

NCAA tournament had become by 1963, changing drastically from the time Ben Hilbun tallied it in 1959.

In the nearly half century since, the story of the '63 team has been sensationalized. But William Winter, the former governor and perhaps the state's most respected statesman in retirement, did not hesitate when asked if the team's trip was as important then as it's made out to be today. "Absolutely," he said, barely letting the question end.

As the 50th anniversary of the 1963 game nears, Mississippi State has sought to embrace the team's impact. In recent years, it has hosted reunions of the various teams involved, including a 2011 event for all of Babe McCarthy's players on the occasion of his banner being raised. In 2011–12, when State commemorated one hundred years of basketball, Howell was named to the school's all-time starting five, and the 1963 Loyola game was named one of the top five games in the school's basketball history. Two documentary films, including one shown in conjunction with a NCAA tournament regional in Detroit in 2008, were made. A lengthy *Sports Illustrated* article was published in 2003. On the occasion of the NCAA's 100th anniversary in 2006, the Loyola–Mississippi State game was named one of the twenty-five defining moments in that organization's history.

"It would have to be, without question, in the top five athletic events in the history of Mississippi State athletics," said Larry Templeton, the former athletic director. "And probably, the significance of what it meant and how it was handled, probably in the top five events in the history of the university."

And the basketball itself? For half a decade in a time when Mississippi needed it most, Mississippi State's basketball team ruled the South.

"When you look back to see what he did—I mean, Adolph Rupp dominated college basketball. Not just the SEC, but college basketball in general at this time," Hutton said. "And you look at what Coach McCarthy did. He took a bunch of guys—and Brookhaven was the largest town that any of our players was from…He took a bunch of little old country guys, small-town guys, and four out of five years he wins the SEC championship. And should've went to the NCAA Tournament."

NOTES

CHAPTER 2

1. Ballard, *Maroon and White*.
2. Biennial Report, Mississippi Board of Trustees of State Institutions of Higher Learning from July 1, 1955, to June 30, 1957, to the State Legislature.

CHAPTER 3

3. Arlie W. Schardt, "Secrets of Auburn's Shuffle," *Sports Illustrated*, December 11, 1961.
4. Hilbun papers, Drawer 1, 348.
5. Hilbun papers, "Basketball Tournament—1959—Don't Let Them Go in State," Box 350.
6. Ibid.
7. Hilbun papers, "Basketball Tournament—1959—Let Them Go (Out-of-State)," Box 356.
8. Hilbun papers, "Basketball Tournament—1959—Let Them Go (In State)," Box 357.
9. Hilbun papers, "Basketball Tourmament—1959—Do Not Let Them Go," Box 351.

CHAPTER 4

10. Colvard, *Mixed Emotions*.
11. Ibid.
12. Ibid.
13. *Sports Illustrated*, December 11, 1961.
14. *Sports Illustrated*, "Scorecard," February 13, 1961.
15. Colvard papers.
16. Colvard, *Mixed Emotions*.

CHAPTER 5

17. Colvard, *Mixed Emotions*.
18. Ibid.
19. Hines, *Bob Walkup Storybook*.
20. Colvard papers.
21. Ibid.
22. Colvard, *Mixed Emotions*.
23. Ibid.
24. Ibid.
25. An earlier draft of Colvard's statement reveals some insight into how he fortified it before its release. In the third paragraph, he inserted "many" to modify "interested alumni and friends." The draft had his key phrase "unless hindered by competent authority" in parenthesis. Colvard placed a bracket around the fifth paragraph but crossed it out; did he debate removing the entire paragraph? In the seventh paragraph, Colvard inserted "well-trained" to modify "young people of Mississippi." And in the final paragraph, in between the two sentences, a sentence reading, "My trust is that Mississippi will be placed in a favorable light nationally," was crossed out and omitted from the final version.

CHAPTER 6

26. Ibid.
27. Eagles, *Price of Defiance*.
28. The *C-L* was right, even if it was wrong in fearing it. In a decade's time, the major athletic teams at both Mississippi State and Ole Miss would be fully integrated. Soon after that, black athletes became the majority on teams.
29. Colvard, *Mixed Emotions*.
30. Colvard papers, "Athletic Dept.," 1962–63, NCAA Basketball Tournament.
31. Ibid.
32. Colvard, *Mixed Emotions*.
33. Ibid.
34. Ibid.
35. Ibid.
36. Mississippi State 51, Loyola (Illinois) 61, Sports-Reference, http://www.sports-reference.com/cbb/boxscores/1963-03-15-loyola-il.html.
37. Colvard papers.
38. Ibid.
39. Ibid.
40. Colvard, *Mixed Emotions*.

CHAPTER 7

41. Ballard, *Maroon and White*.
42. Hines, *Bob Walkup Storybook*.
43. John Feinstein, "That Was Then This Is Now," *The National*, March 5, 1991.

BIBLIOGRAPHY

This work is based largely on a series of interviews with participants and contemporaries of the Mississippi State basketball teams of the late 1950s and early 1960s that were conducted by the author between 2010 and 2012. Information from various media guides also helped establish the timeline. The long runs of the newspapers listed below—primarily the work of Lee Baker, Robert Fulton, Carl Walters and others in the *Jackson Daily News* and the *Clarion-Ledger*—were significant. Other sources are cited where they were used in the endnotes. A summary of those sources, along with a list of interview subjects and other primary material, is included below.

ARCHIVES AND COLLECTIONS

Ben Hilbun Papers, University Archives, Mitchell Memorial Library, Mississippi State University, Starkville, Mississippi.

Dean W. Colvard Papers, University Archives, Mitchell Memorial Library, Mississippi State University, Starkville, Mississippi.

Larry Lee Papers, private collection, Jackson, Mississippi.

Team reference and clippings file for 1963, Mississippi State Athletics Department, Starkville, Mississippi.

BOOKS

Ballard, Michael. *Maroon and White: Mississippi State University, 1878–2002.* Jackson: University Press of Mississippi, 2008.

Colvard, Dean W. *Mixed Emotions: As Racial Barriers Fell, a University President Remembers.* Danville, IL: Interstate Printers and Publishers, 1985.

Eagles, Charles W. *The Price of Defiance: James Meredith and the Integration of Ole Miss.* Chapel Hill: University of North Carolina Press, 2009.

Hines, Jane, ed. *The Bob Walkup Storybook.* Nashville, TN: Hart Street Press, 1995.

INTERVIEWS

Jack Berkshire
Gene Chatham
Jack Cristil
Kermit Davis
J.D. Gammel
Rosemary Gold
Jerry Graves
Bailey Howell
Charles Hull
Doug Hutton
Jerry Keeton
Larry Lee
Jim McCarthy
Laverne McCarthy

Larry McKay
Leland Mitchell
Aubrey Nichols
Bobby Nichols
Billy Roberson
Bobby Shows
Simon Spight
Bill Swords
Mary Swords
Larry Templeton
Ted Usher
William Winter
Jimmy Wise
Jackie Wofford

NEWSPAPERS

Atlanta Journal-Constitution
Greenville (MS) Delta Democrat-Times
Jackson (MS) Clarion-Ledger
Jackson (MS) Daily News

Memphis (TN) Commercial Appeal
New York Times
Reflector
Starkville (MS) News
Tupelo (MS) Journal

OTHER REFERENCE VOLUMES

Auburn University men's basketball media guide, 2012.
Loyola University Chicago men's basketball media guide, 2012.
Mississippi State University men's basketball media guides, 2010–2012.
Ole Miss men's basketball media guide, 2012.
Southeastern Conference men's basketball media guides, 2010–2012.
Tulane University men's basketball media guide, 2012.

ABOUT THE AUTHOR

Kyle Veazey is the sports enterprise reporter at the *Commercial Appeal* in Memphis. There he reports features, investigative stories, sports business news and projects across a variety of subject areas, such as the NBA's Memphis Grizzlies, the University of Memphis, the Big East Conference, Southeastern Conference sports and Memphis's professional golf and tennis tournaments. His November 2011 project on the state and future of the Memphis football program was named one of the top ten sports projects in the nation by the Associated Press Sports Editors (APSE). Before joining the *CA*, he spent nearly five years covering college beats at the *Clarion-Ledger* of Jackson, Mississippi. He lived in Starkville, Mississippi, and covered Mississippi State from 2006 to 2010. He then lived in Oxford, Mississippi, and covered Ole Miss from 2010 to 2011. His first job was covering University of Alabama sports at the *Decatur (AL) Daily* (2005–6). He has won top-ten awards from the annual APSE contest four times and was named the *Clarion-Ledger*'s newsroom employee of the year in 2008.

A 2004 journalism graduate of the University of Mississippi and a native of Henry County, Tennessee, he and his wife live with their dachshund in downtown Memphis.